THE SEVEN
SECRETS of
EFFECTIVE
BUSINESS
RELATIONSHIPS

THE SEVEN SECRETS of EFFECTIVE BUSINESS RELATIONSHIPS

Discover the Power of Friendship

JOHN EDMUND HAGGAI

HarperCollins*Publishers*

HarperCollins*Publishers*
77–85 Fulham Palace Road,
London W6 8JB
www.fireandwater.com

First published in Great Britain
in 1999 by HarperCollins*Publishers*

10 9 8 7 6 5 4 3 2 1

A catalogue record for this book is available
from the British Library

ISBN 000 274061 3

Printed and bound in Great Britain by
Caledonian International Book Manufacturing Ltd, Glasgow

Contents

Introduction

A recent study of 826 US human resources personnel found that about 40 per cent of new management hires failed within the first few months.[1] Asked to give reasons for this high flame-out rate, those surveyed responded as follows:

▌ Inability to achieve the two or three most important objectives of the new job (47%).
▌ Lack of internal political skills (50%).
▌ Confusion or uncertainty about what higher management expects (58%).
▌ Failure to build good relationships with peers and subordinates (82%).

This book takes its cue from that last statistic. Its premise is simple: to be effective in business you need to be good at relationships. Of course you need a quick mind. Of course it helps to have a head for figures. Of course you will benefit from a knowledge of trends and prices. But without an ability to conduct relationships effectively you will not reach your full potential. People do business with people. Being competent in relationships is *the* fundamental skill.

Such is the nature of modern business that we find ourselves on a steep learning curve. Globalism has thrown up new problems of cultural orientation in relationships; there seems to be much less time for relationships, yet also more pressure to get them right; and everywhere, all the time, the rules are steadily changing. Never has it been more difficult to pin down what it means to relate well in business, or to translate principles into sound practice.

This book has very practical origins. For many years my work as Chairman of a globe-encircling leadership training organization has been taking me into every continent and almost every major country of the world. I have had the privilege of working with, and observing at close-hand, some of the greatest business and organizational practitioners of the post-World War II era – from more than 170 nations. And have found myself, as a matter of necessity, forming and maintaining relationships with an enormous range of people in all businesses and professions, up to the top CEOs and members of national governments.

In the midst of all this it occurred to me that being good at relationships requires not aptitude, but a *commitment* to the principle of relationships, and a *determination* to get it right. Although, in a broad sense, almost any of us will say that relationships matter in any organization, relatively few actually *prioritize* relationship-maintenance. And among those who prioritize it, even fewer take seriously the task of acquiring good relating skills.

The seven chapters of the book outline what I consider to be seven skills essential to relationships in every culture and every sector – no matter what the enterprise:

- **SOCIAL INVESTMENT** – the skill of building effective long-term relationships.
- **FACEWORK** – the skill of managing relationships in a way that satisfies another's need for acceptance.

■ **FIRST-LINE FOCUS** – the skill of setting up new relationships.

■ **GLOBALISM** – the skill of making relationships work across cultural boundaries.

■ **MOTIVATING POWER** – the skill of transferring your goals to other people.

■ **NEGOTIATION** – the skill of reaching optimal and mutually beneficial agreements.

■ **CONFLICT UTILIZATION** – the skill of redirecting the energy of conflict.

In each case I have taken a two-stage approach – first looking at the idea, and second seeing how the idea can be applied in practice. I have endeavored to present advice in the form of easily digestible lists, and to anchor discussion in personal experience and documented business and organizational events. At the center of all the skills, however, lies the skill of friendship – and this is where a book on business relating must begin.

Notes

1 Quoted by Anne Fisher, 'Don't Blow Your New Job,' *Fortune*, 22 June 1998, pp.79–80.

CHAPTER 1

Social Investment

What is social investment?

By the 1920s, Elmer Leterman had already attained the undisputed position as America's champion of insurance sales. An article in *Forbes Magazine* said – and it was only half a joke – that when someone created a *Billion* Dollar Round Table, only Leterman would qualify for membership. That's a measure of the man's genius. But strangely, Elmer Leterman – the man who outsold every other broker in the country in the twenties through the early fifties – knew very little about insurance.

His skill – his *passion* – centered on socializing. Talking to Leterman, as I did thousands of times over three decades, you'd have thought business was the last thing on his mind. He seldom brought the topic up unless asked. His tagline was: 'When you think of me, don't think of insurance. But when you think of insurance, please think of me.' Even when someone asked him straight out for a policy he didn't mess with figures – he referred the client to a colleague called Gortz, a green-eye-shade numbers man who was a veritable encyclopedia of insurance knowledge.

In today's world – where margins are narrow and schedules tight – Leterman looks like an enigma. How can such an apparently casual attitude to business actually yield results? Yet we all understand the principle Leterman worked by. In the end, you can't do good business without building good relationships. We see quite clearly from our own experience that the people we're most comfortable dealing with are those who make us feel liked, valued and respected. Benjamin Franklin put it in a nutshell when he said, 'If you want to win a man to your side, first convince him that you are his genuine friend.'

The 'Western Business Style'

The word *genuine* is critical. What we're accustomed to, and what we rightly resent, is being approached with the pretense of friendship by someone whose only interest is to get our vote or our money. For this reason we often meet friendliness with suspicion. We ask, 'What is he after?' and 'What does she really want?' It's not that we don't value friendship, or can't see it as a business asset – we're just so daunted by the task of 'convincing others that we are their genuine friend' that we've got used to working without it. You won't find the word *friendship* in a business lexicon – it's just not in the vocabulary.

Not long ago I was discussing the ideas of this book with a successful executive in the chemical industry. He'd spent a good deal of his life in Switzerland, where his US corporation had established its European base, and had bought and sold petrochemicals across most of the globe. He pointed out to me that in his industry, as in many others, executives have simply got used to relating in short snatches.

'You get to know someone while you're negotiating a deal with him,' he said. 'Maybe you don't see him again for another five or six years. But when you do, you just pick up where you left off. Actually, sometimes you are forced to do some fence-mending in preparation for a satisfactory new business association.'

When I asked him if he made any effort to keep in touch with people between deals, he replied, 'What's the point?'

From this perspective – and it's distinctly Western – a 'business friendship' is the relational equivalent of a bonsai. No one credits it with much potential for growth. The fact that it's possible to 'pick up where you left off' measures how superficial such linkages can be. Trying to know a person in depth will usually be seen as idealistic and impractical. And consequently the Western approach to business has become predominantly task-oriented. We invest in training and techniques. We usually don't invest in relationships – unless we can see the prospect of a short-term payoff. Most of us, if pressed, would say we'd like to put more emphasis on building relationships. We'd also say we're too busy.

How social investment differs from networking

Standing within the Western business world there's a tendency to say that time-pressure and its consequences (both of which are unavoidable) invade business and society in all parts of the globe. But once you move out of the Western hemisphere it's clear that multi-billion dollar business as well as personal career plans can be modeled in a very different way. When *Forbes Magazine* interviewed the Chinese industrialist Robert Kuok, they made the following observation:

> Kuok may not be the biggest player in Asia. We estimate his family's net worth to be at least $7 billion. But for sheer versatility, imagination and ability to get things done, he has no peer.
>
> 'What could take us 18 to 24 months [in China], Kuok's Kerry Group could do in 2 months,' says John Farrell, president of Coca-Cola China Ltd. 'His whole life has been built around building networks with overseas Chinese and in China. The Kerry Group's ability to do things fast is incredible.'
>
> 'I adapt like a chameleon to the particular society where I am operating at the moment,' Kuok says. Robert Riley, managing director of Mandarin Oriental Hotel Group, a fierce Kuok competitor, says: 'He's a local everywhere he goes.'[1]

Relatedness is a feature of Chinese culture – a network across the Pacific Rim known as the *guanxi*. But it is also a product of an individual's own lifestyle decisions. Kuok is 'a local everywhere he goes' not only because he's Chinese, but because 'his whole life has been built around building networks.'

The term *networks*, of course, is familiar in the West. We spend a certain amount of time chatting to people on planes and at conferences, and these contacts, along with those with whom we've had more involved dealings, form the basis of our network. Its concrete expression is usually an ever-thickening file of business cards, an ever-expanding rolodex – in effect, a stack of standing invitations to call people whose services may at some point be useful to us. Usually few of these individuals will know one another. The network operates on the basis of shared goodwill and a tacit understanding that favors asked for will be small – introductions, referrals, appointments for a meeting, and so on.

In summary, network contacts tend to be:

▐ Numerous.
▐ Of low social significance.
▐ Task-driven.
▐ Low maintenance.

These principles of *limited commitment* and *minimum effort* make networking effective. But they also define its limits. For example, if Mr. Jones asks Mr. Brown to introduce him to Mr. Smith, the introduction will carry weight only proportional to the measure of genuine warmth in the relationship between Mr. Smith and Mr. Brown. In the world of networking there may be hundreds of Mr. Browns who have sat next to Mr. Smith on a short hop to Detroit (and have his card to prove it). But finding someone 'close to' Mr. Smith, and persuading that person to help you, is another matter entirely. The *really* valuable connections are made not between network members but between people whose personal links are stronger. Networking, in other words, produces only a skeletal social framework. It gives us a start – but only a start.

In effect, social investment moves a step up from networking, a decision to put some flesh on the skeleton. Like many Chinese, Robert Kuok has been encouraged to make this kind of investment by the culture he was born in. For Westerners it may take more of an effort. Social investment falls far short of a quick fix; we'd more accurately describe it as a discipline, almost a lifestyle decision. It requires a level of proactive concern for others, and sustained, repeated contact – in person as well as by phone, fax, e-mail, teleconferencing and correspondence.

Why social investment works

I have long had a fascination with China, and when the Beijing government reopened the country's borders to the West, I rearranged my calendar to permit a visit. I wanted to achieve something of enduring benefit for the Chinese people – which meant, in the first instance, making contacts inside the country. It began with networking – in fact, with nothing more than a slip of paper bearing the single name Madam Tu Zhen.

I knew that, at the request of the PRC (People's Republic of China) leadership, this Chinese scholar and educator had recently overseen a visit by some of America's Fortune 500 company CEOs, accompanying them from Guanzou to Beijing. She graciously accepted my invitation to tea, and introduced me to her husband, Dr. Mei Lanfang, also a scholar and the son of the founder of the China Opera Company.

The only request I made of Madame Tu Zhen that afternoon was that, if possible, she might introduce me to other key individuals in Beijing. Within 36 hours I had enough meetings to fill up an entire month. Madame Tu Zhen commended me to leaders in the arts, education and professions. She also arranged meetings with equivalent leaders in Shanghai. When I left China, all the contacts I'd met insisted I return – an invitation the Chinese do not extend out of mere politeness.

What turned networking into social investment was my sustained effort to stay in contact with the people I'd met. Over four years and eight visits the connections strengthened, and by 1988 I was able to invite thirty-two key leaders from the PRC to take part in a Sino-American Cultural Exchange which Haggai Institute for Advanced Leadership Training sponsored at Georgia's Lake Lanier.

The first group came under the aegis of the CAAIF (China Association for the Advancement of International Friendship) and included a number of top educators, businesspeople, photo journalists and writers. The second group, this time representing the CAIFC (China Association for International Friendly Contact), included in addition some veteran government leaders and was led by the PRC's first representative on the United Nations Security Council.

It's revealing that, over ten years and twenty-six visits, both government leadership and press in the PRC have referred to me publicly as *lao pengyou* – literally 'old friend.' It reflects the high value the Chinese place on sustained friendship. The Chinese government had no special reason to court my favors. I did not go to China as the president of a foreign power. Nor did I go with money or the promise of lucrative trade deals. I set out – as I have in all my dealings – to convince others that I am their genuine friend. And to do that, I had to go beyond networking.

I think there are three reasons why this kind of social investment works, in any culture:

■ **PEOPLE LIKE TO DO BUSINESS WITH FRIENDS.** This is the simple truth behind Elmer Leterman's success. Custom, information, job appointments and useful contacts are far more likely to come your way if you're linked to a circle of people who know, like and trust you.

■ **PERSONAL ACQUAINTANCE CONFERS ADVANTAGE.** On a level of business psychology, *knowing* people clearly makes a difference. Fisher and Ury's classic work on negotiation, *Getting to Yes*,[2] proposes as the first two steps in the negotiation process: (1) distinguishing clearly between the people you're negotiating with and the issues you're discussing, and (2) focusing on the other party's real interests and not on their stated positions. Neither of these can be accomplished successfully on the strength of a single lunch. Successful deal-making, as well as successful management depends upon a keen observation of the interests and characteristics of those with whom you work. Not in the sense of winning a more powerful bargaining position, but in the sense meant by Fisher and Ury, of achieving real sensitivity to needs and an information base that rests on more than inspired guesswork.

■ **PEOPLE HELP THOSE THEY KNOW WELL**. The stronger your connection with someone, the more they'll be willing to put themselves out for you. Long-term relationships always lead to a sense of mutual obligation – a fund of goodwill accumulated and dispensed in a way akin to capital.

Why we need to target friendships

Most people are 'socially underutilized.' That is, they have a far greater capacity for relationship-building than they ever put into practice. Business, though, often gives the opposite impression. Many people in mid-career wonder how they can even accommodate essential home relationships alongside a busy office life. Like it or not, scarcity of time means we have to choose where we make our social investments.

At this point many of us bite our lips and wonder if 'choosing our friends' doesn't look a bit calculating. It runs against the grain to scan our social horizons and select certain individuals as more 'useful.' But we may as well be candid. In business we naturally seek to cultivate contact with people we can do business *with*. There's no big secret about it; we're not feigning friendship on false pretenses. Every one of Elmer Leterman's contacts knew he sold insurance – but they also knew he was, in Franklin's phrase, their 'genuine friend.' There's no rule that says our friendships have to arise by accident. We have no difficulty with the idea of targeting potential mates. Why should it bother us to target potential friends?

One reason people don't target others for friendship is a fear of being rejected. They think the other person will be too busy, or that their motives will be questioned. Yet in my experience this rarely happens. As the psychologist and university fundraiser Harold Seymour once said, the most driving desire most people feel is to be *sought after*. When someone stops to ask you directions, you don't feel put upon, you feel flattered – even if you haven't a clue how to help them. Which means – incidentally – that a highly effective strategy in building relationships is to ask for advice. No one minds giving away a little expertise. In fact giving such help makes them feel useful and valued.

Ways to apply social investment

Use good practice in networking

Networking is where social investment starts. It remains fundamental to doing business in the global market, and we should make an effort to get it right. Here's a summary of points to bear in mind when you network:

- **EARS FIRST, NOT MOUTH.** The biggest mistake made in conversation is to speak and not listen. There are good reasons for putting listening first. One, if your talk dominates the conversation, the other party may find you far less interesting than you think. Two, when you listen, you learn. In short, it pays to let others do the talking.

- **PERSON, NOT PITCH.** The second biggest mistake is to start selling your product or service the moment you open your mouth. This is a serious *faux pas*, and will be noted. Even if you've figured out the person you're talking to is a potential customer, keep your powder dry. You need only say enough to make yourself relevant and likeable. If specific business matters come up, try to be oblique, not pushy. There's a world of difference between 'Yes, we offer a strong range of semi-conductors for that application' and 'I'm sure we have exactly the semi-conductor for your application. I'll call you tomorrow and give you a price on it.' Concentrate on making a good general impression, leaving any explicit reference to future contact until it's clear that grounds exist to make it worthwhile. Meanwhile the keynotes are relax, listen, enjoy.

■ **WATCH YOUR WATCH.** Time is precious, so don't squander it. Conferences often allocate time for networking, but they only allocate so much, and there will always be more people around than you can introduce yourself to. So don't pin people down (or let them pin you down) for more than five minutes unless there is some good reason for continuing the conversation. It's perfectly acceptable to affirm how pleasant it's been to talk. If it's true you might say, 'I'd like to know you better,' and then move on. Of course if you're stuck on a ten-hour long-haul to Tokyo, there's a little more leeway – but even here, remember to keep it snappy. People have other things to do on planes besides chat.

■ **CARD REQUESTS GO DOWNWARDS.** Remember the protocol on exchanging cards. When talking to someone of higher rank, it's good practice to offer your own card (so long as the situation warrants it), but *not* good practice to ask for his or hers. Executives who see value in keeping a connection with you will not be stupid enough to let you slip away. If they don't take the initiative, there's no point in pushing it.

■ **FOLLOW-UP INTELLIGENTLY.** The whole point of networking encounters is to lay the ground for future interaction. Irrelevant contacts you filter out; relevant ones you follow up. The rules here are: (1) Follow up before the other person forgets he or she met you. (2) Refer back to your initial meeting. (3) Only call if you're confident they can benefit from knowing you – in other words, don't waste their time. And (4) keep their options open by suggesting a lunch or breakfast meeting that they can, if they wish, politely refuse.

■ **ASK FOR A REFERRAL.** Best used at a second meeting, this simple request can work wonders. It makes few demands on the other person; it can be mildly flattering to them, and very useful to you. You don't have to make a meal out of it. 'Can you recommend anyone else I should be talking to about this?' will do fine. Often a name will come up immediately. If not, let the request drop, and move on to something else.

Build a social investment portfolio

Somebody asked me recently how many friends I keep in touch with on a month-by-month basis. When I got down to counting them I realized there were well over a hundred. Of course no two relationships are exactly the same. Some I interact with much more frequently – many two or three times a week, and in one instance once and sometimes, virtually every day. Others I call perhaps once a quarter. This takes effort. On average I'd say my investment in relationships takes up something like twenty hours a week. And that's not cold-calling potential donors, or drumming up business. That's just maintaining a 'portfolio' of existing friendships.

If that looks like a large slice of your working week, I'd direct your attention back to Elmer Leterman. Maintain your relationships properly, and when someone has business to do he'll go to you, not your competitor. Social investment produces a confidence, an understanding, a rapport, that networking alone cannot match. *Forbes Magazine*, for example, commented on the speed with which Robert Kuok's connections could help implement a business plan. It also noted that Kuok had been building these linkages for decades. But you don't have to have made a social investment for thirty years before you see a return, and the principles covered in the remainder of this chapter help to put the process on a fast track. These are as follows:

- Keep investments active.
- Interact with a purpose.
- Don't manipulate.
- Be a 'link-broker'.
- Think broad and long.
- Don't bore people.
- If you're not a 'natural' – push yourself.

Keep investments active

This requires more than just sending Christmas cards. A relationship that consists of an exchange of cardboard once every twelve months isn't going anywhere. You're letting the other person know you're still alive – *and that's it*. Strong relationships don't begin or flourish by accident. Someone has to initiate them. You will not find this difficult – but unless you have an unusually capacious memory, it will require some organization.

The key points are these:

- **SET A TARGET GROUP.** Actually write down names. Tell yourself, 'These are the people I'll begin by making a particular effort to stay current with.' Some of them may already be in your circle of close contacts; others may not. Making the list doesn't mean closing it – you can always add others later.

- **SET A BASELINE.** Decide what minimum level of contact you're going to keep up. Say, once a quarter. Again, you will deal with some people on your list far more frequently, but the baseline should reflect what you can reasonably manage for the whole group. Don't be over-ambitious, but don't undersell yourself either.

- **KEEP A RECORD.** Keep a log of your contacts with the people on your list. If something important is about to happen in somebody else's life, make sure you note it in your diary. Set reminders on days a certain person needs a call. Try to be aware of what's going on with others, and how you can provide positive support for them without smothering them or being intrusive.

■ **FIND A RHYTHM.** Try and build a natural rhythm for contact, rather than relying on 'clockwork' calls. If someone's going to spend three weeks in Latin America, for instance, give him or her a couple of days to get over the jetlag, then phone up and ask how it went. Good timing can speak volumes: the right moment, for the right duration. If they come to visit, have flowers or a fruit basket in their hotel room to greet them.

■ **BE FLEXIBLE.** Don't feel you have to treat everyone the same. People have different schedules. Some have families. Others spend every spare hour at work. Be supportive without getting in the way.

E-mail has established itself as a pain-free way of keeping in regular contact. For details on this, see the next chapter. Meanwhile a word of warning. E-mail is *so* easy to use that you can end up getting too much of it. The 'quick note' that downloads with fifty others won't always make the impression you hope for – particularly if it has nothing of substance to say.

In the end there is no substitute for meeting others face-to-face. A television evangelist once tried to tell me that TV had outstripped all other communication media as a means of persuasion. Though not blind to the powers of TV, I asked why in that case he ever bothered to speak in public at all. Why not just send a video tape? The answer's not difficult to see: in a relationship nothing takes the place of actually being there. No amount of teleconferencing can reproduce the feeling of sitting around the same table.

In the end, social investment cannot be done purely on the basis of indirect media. Once you've met someone a few times and you've come to know each other, the telephone provides a good way to stay in touch – and is often much more personal than e-mail. And of course there's nothing wrong with using two media back to back – placing a phone call, then following through with an e-mail or fax so the other person has something on file. Without being intrusive, the follow-up also acts as a gentle reminder of what was discussed.

Interact with a purpose

I define close friends as people you can afford to 'waste time with.' But when you're building a relationship you need to observe the basic courtesies. Other people are busy, just like you are. They have a day's work to get through. Your call, or your visit, will be welcome only so long as it makes an enjoyable and relevant addition to their day. So when you contact someone, always

1 Make sure you have a reason.
2 Ensure that reason has value to the other person.
3 Be focused and concise.

Calling without cause will give the impression you are over-attentive or, worse still, insufficiently occupied. Calling for the wrong reason will irritate. Being vague and verbose will make your next communication less welcome – as will communicating too often. You won't find any hard figures to apply in any of this; everyone's different. The burden rests on you to judge it right. The one thing you can bank on, though, is the sense of gratification you'll produce by being genuinely considerate.

Being considerate indicates you're being professional – not crowding people, thinking through what you want to say to them before you open your mouth. But it also involves taking the time to listen. It's amazing what you can learn about someone from even a short exchange. A relative is ill. A child is going to boarding school. He likes hill-walking in Nepal. She's about to change residence. With a little discipline – and a pen and pad, or a palm-top – you can keep a note of what's happening in another person's life, and gear your communications accordingly. And usually you can do a lot better than sending the standard birthday card. You'll make a big impression, for example, just with an unprompted reference to a remark the person made in your last conversation. 'Hi, how are you?' is fine; 'Hey, how did you get on in Berlin?' adds personal interest and a touch of class.

It takes a little homework, that's all. Most of us spend a few minutes of the day keeping up with stock prices or sport. We can easily spare a few minutes for our social investments. Usually I go through my records about once a month to prepare for the next month's contacts I need to make and people I need to encourage and assist. It doesn't have to be a big deal: a newspaper article, a piece of business information, a call before they go in for surgery. And don't be satisfied with gestures. When somebody's sick, send flowers two or three times, not just once. Continuity matters. A single card, a single bunch of daffodils – it's nice, but it's also a token. The *second* contact – the one that says 'I'm still with you, keep hanging in there' – gives a real lift. And it doesn't break the bank or make intolerable demands on your time.

Don't manipulate

Business can easily narrow our focus to the short-term payoff. Charities, for example, have been known to send out 'free' packs of Christmas cards in the hope that this will engender a sense of obligation and make you send them money. Sometimes it works. But it's a plain fact that people don't want to buy or give simply to repay a favor. They'll feel manipulated and justifiably resentful. Even if they comply once, they probably won't do it again.

There's no equivalent of a futures market in social investment; by its very nature it's long-term. All relationships involve giving and receiving, and all relationships result in some sense of mutual obligation. But a focus on end-benefits will reduce relationship-building to a kind of softening-up process, a calculated injection of goodwill designed only to influence another person's future decisions. And that will fail for three reasons:

1 You have no real interest in the relationship itself.
2 The other person will soon detect your insincerity.
3 You will soon give up.

If you think of end-benefits at all, think of end-benefits to the *other person*. In any kind of business approach, make it a rule to give the balance of advantage to the recipient. If the other person ends up saying, 'Ah, now I see what he really wants,' you've messed up. Now, you may think this sounds coy coming from someone running a not-for-profit leadership institute, much of whose work could be described as 'going round asking people for money.' But the fact is I wouldn't make any kind of pitch about Haggai Institute if I didn't feel it amounted to a genuine and life-enhancing opportunity for the potential donor. On occasion I've been known to ask for gifts straight out. But even then there's no pressure, no hidden agenda. I'm giving information, giving support, giving time, giving opportunity. Even with established donors, if I think their involvement doesn't enrich them I'll say, 'I don't want you to stay with the program if it makes you uncomfortable.'

For example, at dinner in London one of my UK directors told me he was heading for a nervous breakdown. He sat on over 100 boards! Three times a month he made a London–New York round trip. He was the largest UK donor to our organization at the time. He had arranged for us a prestigious office at Berkeley Square.

I told him candidly that he needed to get off most of the boards, reduce his travel and reassess his priorities. He looked me straight in the eye and said, 'What would you think if I told you I must resign from your board?' I said, 'If your conscience so leads you, you must resign.' His resignation left a big hole in our UK leadership. His scaling down of his global operations reduced his giving to our organization by thousands of pounds sterling annually. But I retained his friendship. In fact that response strengthened our relationship.

Be a 'link-broker'

For years, Elmer Leterman kept a table at the Algonquin Hotel in New York City. He brought three guests every time he dined there – usually five lunchtimes a week – making sure that each guest wanted to meet the other two. Hundreds, maybe thousands of people sat at Elmer Leterman's table. That's what they called it: Elmer Leterman's table. And when they tore down the Algonquin, Leterman moved to the Four Seasons where a reserved table with a gold plate bearing his name occupied the most advantageous location in the restaurant. Also, he always had his professional photographer on hand to take a picture of the quartet. Each guest received a photo with at least two people he was proud for visitors to the office to see him with. And, in the middle of every one sat Elmer Leterman – larger than life!

Why did he do it? My guess is that it added a new dimension to his relating. Having so many close contacts, he took a delight in introducing them to each other. He knew them all well. He was a discerning man. He could tell which personalities would hit it off, and whose professional interests might profitably combine. He got a buzz from playing the role of facilitator. And it worked because, of course, people love invitations to events they consider important. They love to be sought after. And someone with a genuine interest in his friends can more or less guarantee that the event will result in the satisfaction all round.

I've never kept a table at a hotel. But the more extensive my social investments have become, the more often it occurs to me that Person A and Person B, whose paths would naturally never cross, would both benefit from meeting each other. Maybe one has a product or expertise the other needs. Maybe they operate in related professions. Either way, all it takes is a little attention and thought. And there are very few individuals well-enough connected to be able to bring others together constructively. It puts you in a rare position – and you'll find it enormously satisfying.

Think broad and long

Western business people often make two mistakes in the way they plan relationships.

First, we fail to think long-term. In a wider sense this has direct repercussions for the strength of our businesses. For example, the place of continuity in business connections in Far Eastern culture, particularly among the Chinese, has not been sufficiently grasped by Western corporations. A company trying to get a foothold in the Pacific Rim operates at a severe disadvantage if it constantly replaces its contact staff. If people assigned to Singapore one year are transferred to Mexico City the next, the company loses touch with friends developed by the original group. Because individuals lose touch, corporations find it more difficult to sustain long-term economic cooperation.

But the problem impacts on us as individuals also. Promotion and job mobility produce a constant relational turnover and pressurize us into cutting off old relationships to crowd in some new ones. We don't take the trouble to 'keep up,' and so we don't reap the rewards. Also, we end up with social networks with far more horizontal than vertical elements – that is, we relate far more strongly to our peers than we do to our seniors or juniors. We fail to think 'broad' in our relationships, constantly returning to our own social type and our own age-bracket to replenish our friendships as we get older and move around.

So part of effective social investment must be to ensure that we persist in relationships even when distance intervenes, and that we relate effectively 'up and down' as well as 'across.' You need not break social taboos to do that. If you feel you're losing touch with the younger generation, get to know your friends' children or grandchildren. Relationships that take you out of your familiar world can be among the most enriching.

Don't bore people

'When you think of insurance, please think of me,' said Elmer Leterman. Well, Leterman may not have pushed insurance at his friends, but he had a hundred and one ways of making sure he stayed at the forefront of their minds.

If you've ever tried hailing a cab on a rainy day in New York, you'll know you might as well forget it. So Leterman made a point of giving out gold-plated whistles, wrapped in a note that said, 'For your taxi in the rain.' He was constantly handing out books and write-ups – anything he knew would be of interest. Not once would he forget your birthday. And he had a great sense of humor. If he hadn't seen you for a while he'd send you a business card so small you could hardly see it. And when you put your glasses on you'd find it said:

> [Elmer G. Leterman]
> Due to your lack of business I've had to resort to economy cards

It was perfectly judged.

Of course nobody can teach you humor. But if you have a sense of humor, use it. Doing things that are unusual and amusing – without putting anybody down – will guarantee to get you remembered. In the often strait-laced world of business, brightness makes an impression – and it doesn't take a gift of the gab or a talent for telling tired jokes in a hotel bar.

If you're not a 'natural' – push yourself

Leterman's great advantage derived from his genuine love of people. That's what made him his fortune. And frankly I don't know of anyone with money like that who hasn't a capacity for relationships – that's how integral friendship is to business. But not everyone has a natural affinity for relationships. What if you're 'not a people person' – can you improve your business relating? The answer is definitely yes – for two reasons.

First, social investment is a *discipline*, not a genetic disposition. It has nothing to do with your natural abilities. You may love company and positively dislike being on your own. Or you may basically be a loner and find socializing a bit of an effort. It doesn't matter. You can improve your management of social contacts, and you can train yourself to take some of the uncertainty out of social interaction. Unless you're a pathological recluse, practice helps.

Second, I know from personal experience that shyness can be overcome. Most people would describe me as naturally sociable. But I'll be straight with you: I am not a natural at anything I do. As a teenager I was so shy that my dad threatened to deprive me of the use of the car if I wouldn't come out in the living room and say hello to visitors. That's how bad I was at relating. I got to *nineteen* years of age before I had the courage to ask a girl out on a date. I always liked people – but actually dealing with them socially I found incredibly difficult. What made the difference? Initially, I think, just attitude – I forced myself to be sociable.

My younger brother Ted, who ended up designing some of America's most sophisticated satellite systems, once told me he wanted to meet the head of the Tennessee Valley Authority – a big dam project. I had no idea who the man was, but I made it my business to find out. Several friends said they'd get me an appointment, but none did, and in the end I called and did it myself. Then I took Ted up to see him. I shook the CEO's hand and said, 'Mr. So-and-so, this is my brother Ted. He's a scientist with a first-rate mind, and he has great dreams and concerns ...' And so on.

A few weeks later my father told me Ted had been amazed. He'd said, 'How could John just walk into that man's office and be comfortable with him? How does he do it?' Well it wasn't natural ability, that's for sure. My father hit the nail on the head. He told Ted, 'John determines what he has to do. When he's done that, the thing's no longer an option. It becomes a mandate, and he does it.'

Which is about right. If you have to do something, you may as well give it all you've got. And here's the remarkable thing: even when, like me, you feel shyness like lead weights in your shoes, the more you force yourself to socialize and take initiatives, the more you learn the ropes and the easier it becomes. Just like anything else, you can learn it.

Summary and action plan

You are never going to hit your potential without people. It makes no difference how big your product is, how essential your service is. People do business with people, not with companies and corporations. If someone doesn't enjoy doing business with you – it doesn't matter who you are – as soon as someone else comes down the pike with a product or service as good as yours, he'll take his business to that other person. At the end of the day it's just that simple. So it's good business to relate well. In fact it's stupidity not to.

In the Western world 'relating well' is generally taken to mean networking and a facility for running short-term relationships. The limitations of this as a way of conducting business relationships becomes apparent when we compare Western networks with Eastern ones, in particular the Chinese *guanxi*. Though business in the East has a very different social context, many of its advantages can be realized if networking is regarded not as an end itself but as a first step to the construction of stronger, long-term business relationships – in other words, social investment.

This makes social investment much more than a management technique. Because it implies a particular set of values, and involves certain attitudes and priorities in business relating, it demands considerable commitment. Applied piecemeal, or only at given times and for given periods, it will do little good. Making social investment work in business relating, then, requires us to take a number of definitive steps, which could be summarized as follows:

1 Audit your relationships. List the individuals – apart from close family – who form your 'inner circle' of social links.
2 Decide who else you want to take the time to forge stronger links with. Are any of your existing or proposed connections cross-generational?
3 Ask what minimum level of contact you would plan to maintain with your close links.
4 Look at the methods you use to keep in touch with people, and ask how well they meet the needs of the relationships. Is it possible to ensure that some of your meetings take place face-to-face?
5 Find a convenient way of logging your meetings with others and keeping track of what is happening in their lives. Build important information into your own scheduling.
6 Once a month arrange to spend a few minutes reviewing your log, making sure your calls are up to date and your links are in good order.

Notes

[1] Andrew Tanzer, 'The Amazing Mr. Kuok,' *Forbes Magazine*, 28 July 1997, p.91.
[2] R. Fisher and W. Ury, *Getting to Yes* (Boston: Houghton Mifflin, and New York: Penguin, 1981).

CHAPTER 2

Facework

What is facework?

A recent survey in the Italian magazine *Riza Psicosomatica* revealed an interesting fact. According to the researchers, 70 per cent of Italians confessed to telling between five and ten lies per day. 'Don't worry about it, it's all been taken care of,' was the most common, closely followed by 'I know all about that' and 'I'll always love you.'[1]

The problem, of course, isn't exclusively Italian. 'I'll always love you' may not be heard often in corporate offices. But 'Don't worry about it, it's been taken care of' definitely has. In fact it's heard almost every day, almost everywhere. Another one is 'It's almost finished.' Still another, 'I'm sorry, my train was late.' And yet another, 'I don't know why it hasn't arrived, I posted it two days ago.'

Lies, it seems, have become an integral part of business relating. In most cases it's not because people have any intention of subverting standards or ruining good practice. Most lies of the kind shown here are told because telling the truth would show the person up in a bad light. He says, 'It's been taken care of,' but he means 'I'll do it soon.' He says, 'My train was late,' but he means, 'I missed the train because I stopped to buy a packet of cigarettes.' And so on.

In these situations the liar asks others to accept an 'enhanced' version of himself that differs substantially from the real person he is. In reality he is a forgetful and disorganized individual who lets deadlines overrun and can't face a journey to work without cigarettes in his pocket. Sensing that this will not endear him to others, however, he presents his 'enhanced' version, in which he is efficient, hard-working and a victim of circumstances beyond his control.

This 'enhanced' version is called a 'face.' You don't have to be a liar to have one. We all negotiate our relating by use of a face. We all present versions of ourselves that are better than we actually are. We all have to cope with 'face-threats' – that is, embarrassing incidents that could result in our 'losing face' and having our 'unenhanced' selves revealed. And to a remarkable degree we all cooperate in keeping face-threats at bay.

Take that employee who says, 'Don't worry about it, it's been taken care of.' Any manager with half an ounce of savvy will know what's going on. But in most situations they're unlikely to call the person's bluff. Doing that would occasion a face-threat – in other words, force the person to admit he's fibbed and subject him to the stigma of shame. Showdowns take a toll on human relationships, and managers will often prefer the lower-risk option of accepting the reassurance – not because they believe it, but because attention has already been drawn to the problem, and there's a good chance the employee will take the hint.

Facework – the effective negotiation of face-threats – is probably one of the most essential and at the same time most underrated skills in business. How you handle face influences your power to motivate others, your ability to keep relationships sweet, and your dexterity in handling sensitive negotiations without causing needless offense. Face is a game we all play. Its aim is simple enough – to avoid embarrassing one another unless absolutely necessary. What makes it tricky in the global marketplace is that different cultures play by slightly different rules.

Face in Western business

Facework in Western business, as in Western relationships generally, takes two forms:

- Supporting 'reputation face' – that is, other people's desire to be liked, valued and respected. This is sometimes called positive facework.
- Supporting 'freedom face' – that is, other people's desire to be free from constraint and imposition. This is sometimes called negative facework.

Doing these things is what we mean by 'being polite.' We do *reputation* facework whenever we praise colleagues, reward their competency, and show ourselves to be in solidarity with them. An example is the managerial technique of couching criticism in affirmation. For instance, 'You've done some good work in sales, and I'd like to discuss ways you can further improve your overall performance.' At the same time, we do *freedom* facework whenever we act in a way that respects a colleague's space and avoids making invasive demands on his or her privacy or schedule. We all sense the difference between barging in on someone, and leading with an opener like, 'If you have a moment today I'd like to discuss ...'

Well-executed facework averts face-threats and keeps relationships sweet. The particular problem in business, though, is that some management situations demand face-threatening action. An example comes up in a book on the buyout of RJR Nabisco in 1988. Bryan Burrough and John Helyar paint a bleak picture of the old Nabisco corporation:

> The Coppers-era bakeries were deteriorating, and Nabisco no longer had the profits to modernize or replace them. Even after Bickmore retired in 1973, little changed. In the seventies Nabisco was run by decent, slow-moving executives who fostered a culture that venerated past glories. Good men all, but change agents they

weren't. As one of its ad agency executives put it, 'How could somebody who makes Oreos be mean?'[2]

Almost certainly, the kind of action required to rescue Nabisco could not be taken without putting someone's nose out of joint, and in keeping with the times a management culture broke in on the company that came near to making face-threats a virtue. Burrough and Helyar describe in detail the head-rolling turn-around imposed on Nabisco by Ross Johnson and his colleagues – a Rambo-style approach to business relating much-lauded in the eighties and which still holds an instinctive appeal in some quarters of corporate America. 'We were charging through the rice paddies, not stopping for anything, taking no prisoners,' recalled strategist Henry Kravis, as though the subsequent buy-out were a rerun of Vietnam.

Such thinking – as the analogy suggests – is essentially antagonistic, and depends ultimately not on forging cooperation but on acquiring sufficiently massive amounts of power. Glamorous it may be; but it is not the way most day-to-day business can be run, nor is it effective in any situation where relationships have to work long-term. Tough decisions need more attention to face – not less.

And it doesn't need a corporate crisis to produce face-threats. These arise regularly in the normal running of a management structure. Almost any interaction – orders, advice, requests, offers, promises, compliments, criticism, disagreement – carries a potential face-threat, and in the West an elaborate array of facework strategies has grown up to forestall this. Facework does not imply softness, or a reluctance to take hard decisions, or an insistence that social goals should automatically be placed above financial ones. Properly done, however, it *does* input significantly in the maintenance of good working relationships, and limit unnecessary fallout when hard decisions have to be taken. Wherever possible, it keeps people on your side.

Face in Japanese business

Most business people who've had dealings with Japan will tell you that face-saving is, if anything, more important to the Japanese than it is to Westerners. This is probably true. It's important to recognize, though, that face in Japan has distinct – and different – connotations.

In the West, your face has to do with your rights as an individual – your right to be accepted for what you present yourself to be, and your right to defend your territory from the encroachment of others. Typically, then, one Western businessperson will greet another with an expression like 'Nice to meet you' – reputation facework that affirms the other person as worth being introduced to.

The equivalent Japanese expression, though, is quite different. A Japanese businessperson might well say *Doozo yorosiku onegaisimasu*, meaning 'I ask you please treat me well / take care of me.'[3] To a Westerner this will seem excessively self-effacing, if not something of an imposition. It only makes sense when you realize that, in Japan, face has nothing to do with preserving the individual's rights, and everything to do with maintaining proper and harmonious links between the individual and his or her social group. It is an honor to be asked to take care of someone, because it credits you with higher social status.

Among the Japanese, harmony depends on recognizing social distinctions, and loss of face will occur on both sides if you fail to acknowledge your position correctly. Thus if someone of the *same* social rank greets you in this fashion, the appropriate response is *Iie, kotira koso* ('No, I am the one who should ask'), whereas if someone of a *higher* social rank makes the greeting, you would use the stronger formula, *Iie, iie, tondemo gozaimasen. Watakusi no hoo koso yorosiku onegai itasimasu* ('No, no, not in the least. I am the one who asks you to treat me well').

Similar distinctions between Western and Japanese styles is present in the way face-threats are averted in the giving of gifts. The Japanese formula *Anoo, tumaranai mono desu ga ...* ('Um, this is a trifling thing, but ...') expresses appropriate deference by implying that the gift may not match the recipient's high standards of taste. At first glance, the equivalent expression in English would seem to be: 'I picked this up in a bargain basement sale – I thought you might like it.' This is polite in a Western context because it reassures the recipient of the gift that he or she need not feel indebted – after all, the gift is only small. Translated into a Japanese context, however, the same remark would appear downright rude. It would say, in effect, 'I bought you this because I think you're cheap'!

Such is the sensitivity to face in Japan that face is often preserved by the use of intermediaries. It is comparatively rare for a Japanese businessperson to make an initial approach without being recommended, since this would increase the risk of face-loss if the approach were rejected.

Ways to apply facework

Pre-empt face loss

Any encounter between business people can result in face-loss. And because effective business will be driven by financial and productivity-related goals, there is always pressure in management to avoid 'pussyfooting around.' In management, therefore, more than other areas of human interaction, you will find yourself in situations where face-threat is hard to avoid. For example:

- During a busy period in the office, your executive assistant unwittingly fails to notify you of a crucial call.
- In a planning meeting, a team member presents a proposal he or she strongly favors but which you know is not going to work.
- You feel a poor decision made by your line-manager has put you in a difficult position. You go to discuss this with him or her.
- You have to make an employee redundant.

All of these situations push you into making what is termed a 'face-threatening action,' or FTA. The prospect looms up of an unpleasant exchange in which you have to deliver unwelcome news. You know the other person will suffer face-loss, and you will prefer to avoid this outcome, both out of regard for the other person's feelings, and because of the long-term damage that might be caused to working relationships. But how can you control face-loss without running away from the problem?

Here are some of the options at your disposal:

■ **NON-VERBAL NOTIFICATION.** There are various grades of response that fall short of a direct, verbal confrontation. For example, pointedly choosing *not* to notice a gaffe made by an employee can often be more effective than spelling it out. Similarly, when somebody's lied to you, the right kind of glance can say 'Come on, we both know you're stretching the truth there' without explicitly threatening the other person's face by demanding a retraction. Not everyone responds to such subtle methods, but the more sensitive the person you're dealing with, the more likely he or she is to pick up on it.

■ **INVITING DIALOGUE.** It's important to recognize the difference between addressing an issue confrontationally ('I'm telling you that's just not going to wash') and inviting another person to open a dialogue ('I could be wrong about this, but my hunch is ...'). In the first you focus on personality, simply bulldozing the other person out of the way. In the second you focus on the issue, allowing the other person to make a reasoned – and dignified – climb-down.

■ **CLAIMING EXPERIENCE.** An example would be: 'I've actually done quite a lot of work in this area, and I came around to the view that ...' You're giving the other person an excuse to be wrong. You know something they don't – something they couldn't reasonably be expected to know. Consequently there's no loss of face for them in going with your view.

■ **THE COGNITIVE DISCLAIMER**. For example, 'I know this may not make a lot of sense, but ...' Or, 'I'm not making the rules here; but company policy clearly indicates that ...' In both cases you distance yourself from the face-threatening criticism, and allow the possibility of the other person's view being reasonable without being appropriate. Watch out, though, that you don't end up taking the wrong side.

■ **PLEAS TO SUSPEND JUDGEMENT.** Face-threatening encounters often ignite because one party fails to hear the other out. When you're breaking difficult news you might say something like: 'Before you respond, let me give you the whole picture.' If respected, this appeal allows you time to put a balanced case without winding down into knee-jerk recriminations.

■ **AFFIRMING REPUTATION FACE NEEDS.** If there's something good to say, then make sure you say it. Criticism will be accepted and acted on much more readily if it's hedged around with sincere affirmations of the other person's worth. Begin with, 'I want you to know I was really impressed with the way you handled such-and-such. There's just one point that's come up and I'd like to discuss with you ...?' But make sure you mean it. Token praise sticks out a mile – and is rightly scorned.

■ **DEPERSONALISATION**. 'It's nothing personal' is probably one of the most over-used (and most mistrusted) lead-ins a manager can use. It's got that way because people say it glibly and, having said it, feel free to dump whatever personal remarks they wish. Used in the right way, this strategy is much more like the cognitive disclaimer – it focuses attention on the issue, not on the personalities surrounding it. For example: 'I want you to know that this matter does not alter in the least my very high personal regard for you ...'

Shoulder blame

These techniques are all used to cushion face-threats
But of course in business, as elsewhere, face-threatening situations
arise all the time, accidentally and without warning. Such crises
require a kind of facework first aid, often called *corrective* facework.
The embarrassing incidents that occasion this have been given
some picturesque names: pratfalls, gaffes, flubs, *faux pas*, boners,
blunders, miscues and mistakes. Some examples would be:

▪ Turning up for a meeting in slacks and loafers when everyone
  else is in a suit.
▪ Making a hash of a presentation.
▪ Getting publicly teased or criticized.
▪ Losing your temper or bursting into tears.
▪ Blundering in on someone else's meeting.
▪ Having to talk to a colleague who doesn't know he's about to
  lose his job.
▪ Knocking a glass of ice tea over someone at lunch.
▪ A false rumor going around that you're planning to downsize
  your department.

It's worth noting that embarrassment spreads. Most people have
been in a meeting where team member A decides to lecture team
member B on something B already knows. Team member B is
embarrassed because his or her competence is called into question. Team members C, D and E are embarrassed for A, who's dis-
playing poor judgement, and for B as the recipient of A's unso-
licited advice. And even if team member A isn't embarrassed
now, he soon will be when someone interrupts him.

This 'spreadability' of embarrassment is one reason why
groups usually cooperate in saving face. In such a situation, B, C,
D and E may tacitly agree to ignore the incident. Alternatively, C,
D or E may try to defuse the tension with humor. Failing that,
someone – usually the team leader – will be forced to intervene,
allowing B to save face at A's expense.

We negotiate such minor face issues routinely in every area of life. In business, though, one kind of 'offense' is particularly prominent, and much more likely to produce division. This is the *professional error.*

It's just a fact that when people work together something will go wrong. And when something goes wrong – even a minor thing – people feel their reputations are on the line. A round of buck-passing begins, and before long everyone is operating in a blame-culture characterized by defensive mental postures, low levels of mutual trust, and a general fear of risk-taking and making mistakes.

At this point face-saving ceases to be a cooperative exercise, and instead focuses on the individual. Energy that should go into the pursuit of creative solutions goes instead into keeping one-self out of the line of fire. People lie to evade responsibility. If lying fails, they make excuses ('It was an accident,' 'I'd been working all night,' 'If such-and-such hadn't happened, I wouldn't have ...'). And if excuses won't wash, they justify themselves by reframing the error in positive terms ('There's no harm done,' 'Other people do this all the time,' 'I thought I was doing the right thing').

In my view, a great deal of trouble could be saved on profes-sional errors if everyone agreed to work by three simple principles:

▮ **KEEP PEOPLE BRIEFED**. If you know something's going wrong, admit it. After all, business boils down to problem solving. No one's going to get angry at you for admitting you need help. They will get angry at you – and with some justification – if you let a problem get out of hand by refusing to consult, or if you fail to keep others informed.

▮ **REMAIN ISSUE-FOCUSED**. What matters in business isn't what an individual has or hasn't done, but what the current challenge is, and how best it can be addressed. Keeping yourself issue-focused – and keeping everyone else the same way – will have the twin effect both of concentrating effort where it needs to go and of diverting attention from wasteful activities like apportioning blame.

■ **USE APOLOGY CREATIVELY.** It's tempting to feel a twinge of self-satisfied pleasure when the other guy's in the wrong. It's also tempting to rub it in a little so they get the message loud and clear. Few things, though, will damage your reputation more than letting other people feel small. If a colleague hasn't performed to your expectations, you'll get far better results – believe it or not – if you lead with an apology. 'Look, I'm sorry, I haven't been keeping up with this project like I planned to. Where are we at the moment?' Apology disarms people. It keeps you in the role of colleague and supporter. And it allows you to keep the focus on the issue, not on the ego of the person you're dealing with. It goes without saying, of course, that if you've made a professional error yourself you should come clean. Believe me, it works.

Don't use up your free passes

All of this the social scientists classify as *reputation* facework. Whether you use if before a face-threat, or after a face-threat, the intention is to prevent embarrassment and loss of reputation or esteem. But in the West, particularly, we also do the other kind of facework – called *freedom* facework – in which the aim is to keep open another person's options.

Simple ways we practice this in the business world include, for instance, giving colleagues the chance to say no. 'Please take my calls while I'm out' is a *freedom* face-threat – that is, it imposes on the other person without asking whether he or she finds it convenient to comply. The 'please' mitigates it to a degree – but only to a degree. Addressed in this rather peremptory fashion, most of us would feel put upon and a little resentful. A politer way of asking would be: 'I know you're busy, but would you mind watching my phone for half an hour?' The request retains its force, but it doesn't block others in. It acknowledges their right to put their own schedules first.

In effect, freedom facework allows us to ask favors without putting each other's noses out of joint. But even with good facework, it's essential to observe the protocol of give and take. According to social scientist Alan Page Fiske,[4] human beings have a fairly sophisticated way of keeping tally of their good deeds. For example, if you agree to watch my phone for me, we both understand immediately that this puts me in your debt. Next time it will be 'my turn' to do a favor. If you are generous and I am busy, you may be willing to do me two or three favors in a row. But the longer this goes on, and the heavier the debt becomes, the more uncomfortable we're likely to feel about it. You're being 'taken advantage of' and I'm not 'pulling my weight.' Put simply: it's not *fair*.

Fiske calls this method of assessing fairness *equality matching*. We unconsciously observe this principle every time we take turns (at getting coffee, for instance) or share out a benefit equally (like splitting a fee fifty-fifty with a partner). And usually we notice pretty quickly if the other person flouts the rules.

Equality matching, though, isn't the only way we assess fairness. Often we do something far more complicated than keep score of who's owing whom. Take the example of fee-splitting. If the first partner in a project does more of the work than the second, they may agree to split *sixty-forty*. On the other hand, if the balance of input shifts – so that the second partner starts to bear more of the load – they'll probably feel the sixty-forty split is now unfair and in need of adjustment. Calculations in this area can get complicated, not least because we're required to put some sort of price on the differing kinds of input people bring to a deal – finance, support personnel, influence, legal advice, trademark and copyright research, as well as acquisition. But the principle stays true – what's deemed to be fair depends on some estimate of comparative value.

Particularly in business, this kind of *market pricing* happens all the time, and is the mechanism we use to assess fairness in all negotiations from wages to mergers. But it doesn't always apply. Within a managerial hierarchy demands are often accepted as fair simply because they come through a recognized authority. Hence phrases like 'the management's right to manage.' Fifty years ago, what Fiske calls *authority ranking* would have had a far higher profile in business. Today, at a time when productivity agreements and wage bargaining have put market pricing firmly at the center of labor relations, the question of what a company can fairly ask of its employees (for instance in terms of flexible working arrangements) has become increasingly controversial.

But Fiske adds one more method of tallying favors – he calls it *communal sharing* – which plays a crucial role in successful business relating. Where communal sharing occurs, keeping tally becomes less important. In fact people do favors for each other 'without thinking,' because they know one another well and all pursue the same goal. There is less anxiety that others will 'free-ride' or take advantage of them. Freedom face-need – the desire to preserve territory, keep options open – gets voluntarily waived.

This dynamic underlies the efficiency of good teamwork. In a well-constructed team, members don't complain about 'doing more than they're paid to' (a conclusion based on *market pricing*), nor will one member feel aggrieved that he or she is 'carrying the load' for others (*equality matching*). They give 110 per cent. Securing fairness becomes a marginal issue when compared to the task of getting the job done. Which – in part – explains why big corporations can be plagued by loyalty-loss and workforce demoralization, while small teams and small production units have generally enjoyed a better reputation for effectiveness and productivity.

Never waste people's time
Another feature of RJR Nabisco's company culture that got short shrift after the arrival of Ross Johnson was the board meeting.

Johnson and the 'Merry Men' he had brought with him from the more dynamic Standard Brands found the format hard to take:

> For one thing, Nabisco's morning meeting began around eight-thirty, in the midst of their hangovers. In contrast to Standard Brands' free-for-all bull sessions, Nabisco's deliberations were carefully choreographed. Executives sat around a table, each making a fifteen minute presentation on a particular cookie or cracker. At the end of each, questions were invited. Rarely were there any; it seemed bad form. It would drone on like this into mid-afternoon, with a break for lunch. Johnson often arranged to be summoned from the room by a phone call, never to return, leaving [his colleagues] Rogers and Carbonell and the others to silently squirm.[5]

Most of us know the feeling of having our precious time eaten up by trivialities. Imposing on people's time creates a freedom face-threat; it limits their freedom of action. And yet it's a besetting sin of business. Every department has its windbag; every corporation endures meetings that are overlong and unrealistically scheduled. Given that you have only seven hours in the average working day, consider these moves to help everyone make the best use of the available time.

First, in the conduct of meetings:

■ **NEVER MEET WITHOUT A REASON**. The word 'meeting' can cover a great many things, from the formal to the completely ad hoc. But even if you're only asking someone into your office for five minutes, make sure your aims are clearly defined. Meetings serve no purpose unless you have something to discuss and decide.

■ **INVITE ONLY THE PEOPLE WHO REALLY NEED TO BE THERE.** Remember people do have other things to do. You wouldn't want your time used up for nothing – so make sure no one else leaves feeling the same way. It's perfectly acceptable to change personnel at time-out. If Miss Smith from Finance only needs to attend for one item on the agenda, do her a favor and make sure that item comes first.

■ **SET A TIME-LIMIT – AND STICK TO IT.** You can usually work out how many minutes will be needed to debate each item on the agenda. Parkinson's Law comes into play at this point: Work expands so as to fill the time available for its completion. Without a preset time-limit, what could be done in 90 minutes may take six hours. If possible, print your agenda out, indicating time-allocations for each item. People appreciate knowing what they've let themselves in for. It's advisable to notify people in writing rather than leave a message on their voice mail. Follow up with a quick call to make sure they've noted it.

■ **GIVE REASONABLE NOTICE.** If the meeting isn't a regular one, don't ask people to bend their schedules out of shape to attend at a last-minute meeting – unless it's extremely urgent. Two days' notice is about right.

■ **DON'T BE LATE.** Add together all the time lost waiting for key people to arrive at business meetings and you'd soon be at the end of the next millenium. Dramatic entrances at five minutes past the appointed hour don't recommend you as a busy person – they confirm you as rude and unprofessional.

■ **SAY AS LITTLE AS POSSIBLE.** Put half a dozen people together in a room and they will – left to themselves – still be there the following morning. It can be an almost overwhelming temptation to chip in on a discussion that doesn't concern you, the effect of which will almost certainly be to further obscure the issue and further delay the schedule. A good rule is to speak only when you have something to say that's germane to the announced purpose of the meeting – and then to be concise.

And as for the telephone:

■ **DON'T BE A PHONE JUNKIE.** Some people seem to derive their entire sense of self-worth from incessant and feverish activity on the phone. You will see them sitting their feet up on the desk, driving with a mobile jammed between jaw and shoulder, or simply walking along the pavement loudly talking into the air. Regarding the use of the phone, you will find benefit in observing the maxim: *Less is more.* Overuse of the phone involves at least three impositions. First, on the recipient of the call, who may not have as much time on his or her hands as you do. Second, on others with more urgent business who are trying to reach either of you (an inconvenience only partly mitigated by voice-mail services). And third, on people in the space around you whose privacy is being invaded by your call. The same rules apply to the phone as to the meeting: do it only with a reason, and keep it short. And know in advance why you are calling, what you will cover, and the conclusion you hope to reach. In his perceptive book *Ten Days to a Great New Life* William Edwards devotes an entire chapter to the 'Pad and Points' technique. He advises the reader to jot down the points to be covered before each phone call, stick with them, and graciously conclude when they're covered.[6]

■ **MINIMIZE YOUR EFFORT.** The first question to ask yourself before you reach for the phone is: 'Do I really need to make this call?' As much as half the time (if you're honest) you'll find the answer is no, and thus will have the opportunity to save a col- league precious time. If the answer is yes, the second ques- tion to ask is: 'Would it be more appropriate to use e-mail or fax?' Remember that written communications stick around in a place outside the other person's memory. This gives the advantage of a greater permanence. Also, the recipient will often find it preferable, because, unlike phone calls, they can be dealt with at a more convenient time. The payback for you is, you're more likely to get a sensible answer.

■ **NEGOTIATE THE CALL UP-FRONT.** For example: 'Hi Amanda, I need three minutes to discuss the June conference. Is this a good time?' Amanda then knows what the score is. If she has three minutes she can get it over with. If not, you can arrange a mutually acceptable time to call back. Resist the temptation to lure Amanda into the call with false promises. Three minutes must mean three minutes. She may forgive you five minutes; fifteen will lose you credibility.

■ **FRANKNESS IS APPRECIATED.** Using the phone doesn't absolve you from keeping promises. If you say, 'I'll call back in a couple of hours,' make sure you do it. Those taking calls for others should avoid parrying callers with queasy half-truths like 'John Brown isn't at his desk right now' (meaning John Brown is busy drinking a cup of coffee), since anyone with half a brain knows exactly what John Brown is doing. And if you say, 'Just give me a moment,' remember how long a 'moment' can seem when you're drumming your fingers and waiting to be connected.

■ **USE ESSENTIALS WHEN MESSAGING.** The essentials are: *who* you are, *when* you called, *what* number you're calling from, *why* you need to make contact (fifteen words or less) and *how* urgently you need a response. Remember: busy people appreciate conciseness; waffling irritates them. And find a formula for signing off that doesn't make you sound like you've forgotten your lines.

■ **RESPOND AT THE SPEED OF SOUND.** Even when others know you're busy, failure to respond to calls quickly will give the impression you regard their business as low-priority. If a colleague calls you, assume it's important, and call promptly even if only to acknowledge the inquiry. Never let the phone go on ringing (you only increase frustration at the other end)

– three rings is the maximum. And if the call is unwanted, try not to get into the habit of cutting the caller off abruptly. Treat all callers with the respect you'd want to be given in their position.

Tame your e-mail

E-mail, it turns out, doesn't solve all the problems of business communication. This is yet another arena in which face-threats can be administered. Indeed, the convenience and distance of e-mail make it peculiarly prone to abuse.

A recent survey of office e-mail users commissioned by the communications giant Novell revealed the following findings:[7]

■ More than half the 1,043 respondents regularly received abusive e-mail, or flame mail.
■ One in seventy claimed abusive e-mail had caused them to change jobs.
■ Men were five times more likely than women to have flamed co-workers.
■ One in six had received official reprimands from superiors via e-mail.
■ 94 per cent said they wasted up to an hour a day dealing with pointless e-mail.

These are staggering figures – not least because they suggest that e-mail attracts and concentrates the kind of face-threatening behavior people would reject if they had to confront each other directly. In other words, the medium itself appears to encourage bad relating. Users employ it regularly to effect both reputation face-threats (abuse, provocation, intimidation) and freedom face threats (spam, frivolous and unnecessary communications).

It's possible, of course, that we have moved into a 'settling down' period of adjustment to a new technology, and that abuses will subside with time. Whether or not this is the case, some lines of consensus are emerging on good e-mail etiquette:

▮ **CLARITY**. One beauty of the e-mail is its brevity. As with all business communication, it's important to be concise. But don't be too concise. You can sound abrupt. Further, replies like 'Yes' and 'No' generally cause confusion if the person you're mailing handles a large volume of e-mail and doesn't recall the exact question to which you're responding. All you'll do is generate an avoidable reply or phone call.

▮ **TAGGING**. It helps recipients if you state clearly in the subject line what the e-mail is about. Avoid vague, frivolous, or ironic tags. Be brief and specific.

▮ **MANNERS**. Flaming and scolding are cowardly. If you have a difference with someone, act your age and confront them directly. If someone flames you, ignore it. E-mail bullies often set out to provoke an irrational response, which they can then copy to others, causing you further annoyance and embarrassment. And remember that all e-mail can be saved on disk, so if you're a victim of harassment you can produce documentary evidence.

▮ **RELEVANCE**. The ease of sending e-mails, and of sending them simultaneously to vast numbers of people, tempts us to communicate irrelevantly. Ask yourself, 'Am I sending this to benefit the recipient, or to benefit me?' If you can't say the former, don't send it. People are busy enough already, without having to sift incoming mail for trash. They will probably delete it anyway if they think it's spam.

▮ **CONFIDENTIALITY**. No e-mail is private. Messages remain on your hard disc even after you delete them. They may be retrieved from other points in a network. Also, once you've sent the e-mail somewhere else, you have lost control of it. The ground rules are: nothing personal, nothing commercially sensitive, nothing embarrassing, nothing libelous, nothing you wouldn't want everyone in the office to see.

■ **SIZE.** Big attachments to e-mails can take a long time to download and use up memory space on the recipient's hard drive. Both can cause irritation and inconvenience. Don't attach materials if the recipient can do without them, or if you can send them more easily in the post. Many times, a few moments of thought and planning will permit you to say all that needs saying in the e-mail opening page without any attachment.

■ **COPYING.** It takes only a few clicks to copy an e-mailed memo to everyone in the office. Ask yourself if they all really need to see it. If not, don't assume they'll be grateful; almost certainly they won't. If you forward mail from elsewhere, it's courteous to clean it up first. Nobody needs to see the chain of links a document has passed down before it reaches them. Such a chain reveals information neither germane nor helpful to the recipient. On one occasion I received an e-mail that revealed a high confidentiality item the sender did not want me to know about – the name and address of a private friend who'd insisted on anonymity.

■ **STYLE.** Just because it's an e-mail doesn't mean you can forget how to write properly. Unless you want the recipient to think you're illiterate, retain the use of capitals to start sentences. Resist the temptation to capitalize whole paragraphs. Use addresses if you need to, open a letter with the traditional 'Dear ...' and finish it with a polite 'Sincerely.' Even if the recipient is a friend in the next office, do him or her the honor of communicating in grammatically complete sentences. You're a professional. Look like one.

Summary and action plan

Facework is not normally thought of as a skill relevant to management and business relating. Yet it remains crucial, because we relate better to others if they see us in the way we would like to be seen. The face, or public image, we present is constantly in danger of being undermined. This sense of shared vulnerability explains why we go to some trouble to help each other 'save face' when embarrassments arise. But we don't always do it. Sometimes we can't be bothered to make the effort. Sometimes we take a perverse pleasure in other people's embarrassment, feeling that it somehow enhances our own image. Sometimes we indulge in destructive behaviors that put others down and damage workplace relationships.

You can't avoid all face-loss. But one of the secrets of good relating is to protect those around us from suffering unnecessary loss of face. Face-saving is not a zero-sum calculation. Making others feel good and valued actually enhances our own reputation, and undermines the culture of blame that so easily bedevils the work environment. Also, in Eastern cultures where face is particularly highly valued, actions that save face for others will have a powerful effect in cementing relationships and developing a sense of obligation.

Facework, then, is a key aspect of business relating that will repay the cost of examination and revision:

1 Review the ways in which face-saving actions by others have benefitted you.
2 Ask yourself what might be some of the positive and negative face-needs of your colleagues and contacts in the world of work.
3 List the situations in which your management responsibilities require you to make decisions that threaten the face of others, and ask how you can more effectively cushion face-threat.
4 Examine the role of blame in your corporate culture, and how this affects working relationships. Ask in what ways you can use apology creatively to defuse tensions.
5 Review your approach to office communications. Determine methods you can employ to neutralize face-threats by improving the handling of e-mails, phone calls and meetings.

Notes

[1] See *Independent*, 9 July 1997.

[2] Bryan Burrough and John Helyar, *Barbarians at the Gate: The Fall of RJR Nabisco* (New York: Harper & Row, 1990), p.32.

[3] This and following examples are taken from Yoshiko Matsumoto, 'Re-examination of the Universality of Face: Politeness Phenomena in Japanese,' *Journal of Pragmatics* 12 (1988), pp.413–26.

[4] See Alan Page Fiske, 'The Four Elementary Forms of Sociality: Framework for a Unified Theory of Social Relations,' *Psychological Review* 99.4, 1992, pp.689–723.

[5] Burrough and Helyar, *Barbarians at the Gate*, pp.32–3.

[6] See William E. Edwards, *Ten Days to a Great New Life* (Englewood Cliffs: Prentice Hall, 1963).

[7] *Shaming, Blaming and Flaming: Corporate Miscommunication in the Digital Age*, reported in the *Daily Telegraph*, 3 June 1997.

First-Line Focus

What is first-line focus?

As a young man, the former ITT boss Harold Geneen joined the recently-launched New York *World Telegram*, to sell classified real estate ads. Two hundred others had been hired on the same terms: $15 per week, plus 10 per cent commissions. The two salesmen who sold the most ads would get permanent jobs on the paper. Geneen later wrote:

> I remember well my first stop to sell a real estate ad to a big adver-
> tiser in Jackson Heights. I had walked a long way to reach him. I
> hesitated a long while before entering his office, fear in my gut.
> But I walked in, drew a deep breath, and blurted out, 'Would you
> like to take out some classified this week in the new *World
> Telegram*?'
> 'No!' he shouted at me.
> 'Thank you very much,' said I, beating a hasty retreat, thankful
> that the ordeal was over.
> As I walked back to the subway, it did not take much imagina-
> tion to realize that that was no way to sell advertising.[1]

Geneen classically mishandled that first meeting. He had allowed fear to dominate him – in other words, he was anticipat-ing rejection before he'd even stepped in the door. His entrance (when he finally made it) was a freedom face threat – that is, he was intruding on the advertiser's personal space and time. And he led with his pitch, making it sound as though he were begging a favor, not offering a benefit. That first line – by which I mean his fatal opening words and all that led up to them – effectively lost him the account.

How we start a relationship is vitally important. Get the opening right, and nine times out of ten the relationship will fly. Get it wrong, and you could be grounded forever – in the timeworn phrase, you never get a second chance to make a good first impression. Much has been written about the first four minutes of a relationship. By far the most crucial interaction, though, occurs in the first four *seconds*. At that 'point of entry' you give out an explosion of signals, verbal and nonverbal, that set the tone for everything that follows. It's a crisis point, because the relationship has yet to be formed and, even with an introduction, you're going in virtually cold. The foundation for the other person's good opinion of you has to be laid down almost instantaneously. And if you fluff it – as Harold Geneen found out – things can crash fast.

Principles of first-line focus

First-line focus, then, is about hitting the ground running when you make a fresh contact. It's also about suppressing the panic reactions that make you 'drop the ball.' Most people know what it's like to forget another person's name almost before the person's finished saying it. Some offer a wet-fish handshake and glue their eyes to the floor. Yet everyone can master first-line focus. Simply act on some hard and simple psychological facts.

■ **OTHER PEOPLE WILL TAKE YOU AT YOUR WORD.**In most first
   encounters, the script is blank. The other person doesn't
   see you coming and say, 'Oh here's so-and-so again, I know
   all about him or her.' Certainly they make preliminary
   assumptions based on your appearance. But unless you drop

some immediate *faux pas* (unzipped fly, smudged mascara, pizza lodged between the teeth) they will give you the benefit of the doubt. And that means it's entirely up to you how you come across. As you step into that relationship your options are wide open – whatever you do at the beginning will be accepted, initially, at face value. If you radiate caution, diffidence and anxiety, that is how others will read you. If you radiate calmness, determination and humor, that is how others will read you. They will accept the 'face' you present – not only because instinctive facework urges them to, but because the information you're giving them is all the information they've got. People tend to place the same evaluation on you that you place on yourself.

■ **OTHER PEOPLE WILL FOLLOW YOUR LEAD.** Whatever you do, or don't do, your presentation of yourself will provoke a reaction. Two people meeting for the first time quickly 'get the measure of one another.' That means the person you're meeting will quickly form a 'working brief' as to what kind of individual you are and what the forthcoming conversation is likely to offer. And that will determine his or her response. To a large degree, therefore, you control the future of the conversation, and by extension of the relationship, by the amount of poise you bring to those first few seconds.

■ **OTHER PEOPLE WILL WANT YOU TO PERFORM WELL.** In Western democratic culture people like to meet 'on the level.' They also like to leave a conversation feeling they've made a worthwhile contact. However diffident you may feel in a first-time encounter, then, it's worth remembering that the other person will usually have positive expectations of you. In such cases he or she will want you to perform well, to be a person worth meeting. And they positively *won't* want you to be a limp rag.

■ **OTHER PEOPLE WILL ACT ON WHAT THEY SEE**. It's an old truism in the communication business that people act on perceptions, not facts. The same applies in first-line focus. Your impact on another person depends not on what you are, nor on what you try to be, but on what he or she perceives you as being. In many cases the practical difference may be small. But again, in first-line focus the initiative lies with you to think through how you're going to come across.

Ways to apply first-line focus

Brief yourself

Too frequently, Western business people go into relationships unprepared. It is the Western Business Style to assume that everyone speaks the 'same language' and that qualities relating to the individual have little significance. Usually we hear about information-gathering in Western business relationships only in the context of aggressive boardroom struggles and hostile takeovers. In such cases the combatants will employ information – preferably private or commercially sensitive information dug up with the help of private investigators and informants – as a bargaining tool to gain strategic advantage.

Apart from all this, though, you need to understand the sound reasons for making the effort to learn. The people you deal with in business will have distinct geographical contexts, which in many cases will differ from your own even if you live in the same country. And the wider the gap, the greater the benefit of informing yourself. It may sound like elementary advice to take a map or a travel guide with you on the plane – but how much do you really know about life in, say, Korea? What's happened there in the last fifty years? Who leads it? What is its economic structure? What recent achievements do Koreans feel proud of? What's happened there in the last week?

If you can't answer questions like these about a place you're about to visit, it's worth doing some homework, for the following reasons:

- Knowing something about other people's cities and nations fosters appreciation, trust and confidence.
- It often brings to light business-relevant information on local culture, office hours and holidays/festivals.
- Good research improves your understanding of the general business conditions in that country or region, and strengthens your awareness of 'where the other person is coming from.'
- It gives you conversational leads.

Once you've found the information, though, be careful how you use it. On a flight not long ago I sat next to an executive bound for West Africa. I have many links with that region, and I asked him how he assessed the country. 'The sooner I get back to Europe the better,' he replied. And then he proceeded to tell me what an awful place he thought West Africa was and what terrible things had befallen him on his last visit. I wondered how he'd come across to his West African hosts.

It's a besetting and all too common sin of travelers to compare the place they're visiting with the place they've come from – and to tell you how much better things are at home. Many such stories get swapped in the departure lounges of Western airports. Amazingly, they are aired just as readily in the hearing of those the traveler has gone to visit. Even if the host politely ignores it (as Eastern etiquette requires), such inexcusably boorish behavior inevitably goes down like a lead balloon, because it's a reputation face-threat.

So if you have to make comparisons, do it in a way that compliments your host region or country. If you have complaints – or even suggestions as to how local conditions could be improved – save them for when you get home. Ideally, try to cultivate enjoyment of new experiences. Certainly in an international setting, there are few better ways to cement a good relationship than to develop a real appreciation for the other person's country and way of life. It's an indirect compliment. Remember, a good conversationalist isn't someone who can tell endless strings of jokes. A good conversationalist is someone who's interested in the world where the other person lives.

Make great first calls

The phone is often your first mode of contact in business. Naturally, all the points made in the first chapter about phone-use in general also apply to making first calls. In addition, bear in mind two more items.

First, you need to find the right person. You may have a name, or better still a name and an introduction. If not, just dial the main switchboard number and talk to the firm's receptionist. Some senior executives will assign that to someone else. Personally I've always preferred to make the calls myself – it makes a far more favorable impression. A good receptionist should know who deals with the relevant business at the relevant level of seniority ('Head of Marketing', or 'The person who deals with service-acquisition for the South-Eastern United States'). He or she will also put you through to that person's office. At this point, one of four things will occur. In order of preference, you will be put through to:

■ The person you want to talk to.
■ The person's executive assistant.
■ The person's voice-mail.
■ The wrong person.

On first calls it's best to avoid voice-mail, unless it's the executive assistant's voice-mail, in which case it is acceptable to leave a brief message identifying yourself, the company you represent, the person you hope to speak to, and a number at which you can be reached. Always remember that the executive assistant is not a military guard; he or she is your *agent*. It's true that part of an executive assistant's job is to buffer and filter incoming calls. But unless you are self-evidently a crank, he or she will help you communicate your business in the most appropriate manner – either by scheduling a future call, taking a message, or recommending you use fax or e-mail. Getting on the wrong side of an executive assistant – showing impatience, disappointment, or unwanted persistence – may thwart your objective. Treating him or her as your friend and professional guide will usually get you where you want to go. Remember, in your target person's office the executive assistant is your best and only advocate. Always take the executive assistant's advice, question intelligently, and never waste his or her time.

So finally the call goes through, and the first-line moment arrives. Here's the checklist for the next few seconds:

■ **IDENTIFY YOURSELF.** For example, 'Good morning, Ms. Smith. This is John Jones of *Corporate Monthly* ...' Don't hesitate, get straight to the point, but keep your voice animated. You're not the police calling to inform next of kin.

■ **ESTABLISH YOUR CREDENTIALS.** If you have an introduction, use it now, even if you've already alerted the executive assistant. For example, '... Ken Brown said I should give you a call ...' Ms. Smith can now breath again, because she knows her good friend Ken Brown wouldn't have referred a lunatic or a double-glazing salesman. She will probably say something like 'Oh yes' to acknowledge the connection. You have won yourself the right to speak – briefly.

■ **NAME YOUR PROPOSAL.** Don't start a long spiel with the aim of softening up Ms. Smith in advance of your close. Almost certainly she will get bored and restless. Instead, zero in on the fact most likely to attract her interest, and say what you're asking her to do. For example, '... We're putting together a feature on key players in the currency markets, and I wondered if you'd be interested in giving me twenty minutes for an interview some time this week ...' If possible, follow up with a sincere compliment. For example, '... I know the

Financial Times has named your company as one of the top performers. Ken Brown tells me a lot of that's attributable to you ...'

▌ **BE GRACIOUS.** By now you've given Ms. Smith every possible chance to say yes. If she says no, she has a reason for it, so accept the rebuff graciously – you never know when you might need to call her again. For example, '... I understand. Thank you for taking the call. It's been a pleasure talking to you ...'

▌ Of course you may be Ms. Smith, taking the cold call from Mr. Jones. If so, try not to bark. People who snatch up the phone and yell 'Yes???' don't inspire confidence. Anyone who's gone to the trouble of dialing your number at least deserves a courteous response. And if Mr. Jones turns out, after all, to be that unwanted double-glazing salesman, don't bite his head off. It may take an extra five seconds to terminate the call without rancor or sarcasm – but it will leave both of you feeling better.

Write great first letters
One of the long-debated questions in business is: *Phone first, or write first?*

In general the answer depends on how well you've done your homework. If you know whom to contact, and know that he or she will find your communication relevant, you may first send a letter or fax, then follow up by phone call (after a decent interval) once the recipient has had time to digest the contents. If you're not sure you have the right person, you may find it more effective to make a short call first. The person won't mind. He or she may well be able to redirect you, and you may find out in five minutes what otherwise could have taken five days.

Preceded by a call or not, the letter must be right. Bear in mind that most people won't sift their daily influx of mail in search of a communication from you – even if you've tipped them off that you're sending it. Everything capable of grabbing that person's attention has to be there in the envelope. You won't be there to explain the letter when it's opened. Those few words you put down are your messenger; they stand in your place. So it's worth getting the basics right:

■ **MAIL OR FAX?** Communicating by snail-mail or courier still has a number of advantages over the fax machine. Chiefly, you can send other, unfaxable things – like brochures – in the same package. Also it allows you to communicate a degree of prestige by using quality stationery. E-mail will increasingly emulate this effect. At present, however, e-mail arrives stripped to the text, and faxes, though they reproduce the company letterhead, often appear as a substandard black-and-white printout. Only in speed of delivery do e-mail and fax have a definite edge.

■ **ENVELOPE.** Letters, of course, come wrapped. If you want to communicate prestige, then, you will have to use elegant personalized envelopes to match your elegant personalized stationery. Avoid using 8.5 by 11 inch (in Commonwealth nations: Letter or C4, and larger) envelopes if smaller ones will do. They may leave your office in perfect condition, but they'll usually arrive looking like half-finished origami. If the material you're sending can't be folded, consider going for a heavyweight or board-backed envelope.

■ **FORMALITIES.** The world of business, especially in the West, keeps moving toward less formality. Once you have estab-lished a relationship you may introduce your letters with 'Dear Joe' instead of 'Dear Mr. Bloggs'. Beware of assuming this intimacy too fast, however. 'Dear Joe' coming from a complete stranger will be a freedom face-threat – an invasion of privacy. If in doubt, go by seniority. Older or higher-placed addressees should be greeted with their titles unless they indicate to the contrary. Otherwise, to strike a balance between stiffness and overfamiliarity, you can always resort to 'Dear Joe Bloggs.' As for closing off, 'Yours sincerely' is now the standard formula for anything formal – and is a must for a first-time approach. One caveat: In Asia, especially in Korea, always use the formal method.

▌ **LENGTH**. Remember that nobody in business has enough time to deal with correspondence. Never try to explain everything in a letter. You want the recipient to act immediately on your request, so state it as briefly as you possibly can. If you put more than half a dozen lines between your 'Dear ...' and 'Sincerely ...' the letter may be consigned to a long wait on the in-tray. Lead with your referral, if you have one. Then follow up briskly with your main point and the *one thing you want the addressee to do*. If other information is needed, supply it on a separate sheet. It may be that you don't want to addressee to do anything in particular, in which case you should clearly mark your letter FYI ('for your information'). If you're not sure what you want him or her to do, don't write.

▌ **APPEARANCE**.Gone are the days of misaligned typewriting. Today word processors produce nearly all business correspondence, so you really have no excuse for a shabby-looking letter. Handwritten notes that say 'Look, I've actually taken the time to write this with a pen' show exceptional attention and regard. But they must be *legible*. Software that uses your handwriting to create a font is effective only if the addressee *thinks* you've used a pen, which means you risk appearing slightly devious. However, even if the recipient has word-processor savvy, the inclusion of personal items that could not possibly relate to anyone else will neutralize the suspicion that you have simply copied the text from somewhere else. Print all letters clearly in a conventional font, with enough space to sign comfortably underneath. And don't let your executive assistant 'pp' your signature. Everyone knows offices are busy, and that bosses aren't always around to sign before the last post. For a first letter, though, it suggests inattention and laziness. Sometimes, I will put in a PS 'Since I will be away when my assistant transcribes this letter, I have asked her, in the interest of time, to sign my name.'

■ **INCOMING MAIL.** You can be a first-time receiver as well as a first-time sender. Everyone has had that call saying, 'I wrote to you last week ...' and then suffered the embarrassment of not being able to remember what the letter said or even that it arrived. Hurried shuffling through the mountain on your in-tray doesn't solve the problem. Maintain and keep up to date an efficient filing system.

Have great first meetings

When you're meeting others, the trick to first-line focus lies in what you do *before* you reach the first line.

Others meet you with certain expectations. Initially these are tentative, and formed on the basis of what they have read about you, what mutual acquaintances have said about you, or what they have gleaned from previous communications by letter, fax or phone. A second and stronger set of expectations arises when a person lays eyes on you. This happens because, in a society where people deal with each other as strangers, we become quite adept at 'reading' each other's nonverbal signals. Intentionally or not, another person will make certain judgements about you based on your:

■ Age.
■ Gender.
■ Build.
■ Posture.
■ Hairstyle.
■ Clothing.
■ Actions.
■ Expression.

If you don't believe it, build up a mental image out of the following components: fortysomething, male, medium-height, slouched, needs a haircut, creased suit, smoking a cigarette, looking like he could use a good night's sleep. Every aspect of your self-presentation will influence the all-important first impression you give to others.

Equally, of course, one may change every aspect of appearance and behavior. Men of a certain age have been known to dye their hair. People work out to achieve a better physique. Most of us stand a little straighter, shine our shoes a little brighter, and pick a few more specks of lint off our lapels, when we meet someone we want to impress. In essence we want to assure the other person that we belong to a circle they feel comfortable with – that we are 'one of them.' We're also trying to win a little recognition for ourselves by appearing to possess attributes – like intelligence, good humor and attractiveness – that others value.

Angling our self-presentation in this way, though, has three drawbacks:

■ **SOME THINGS CAN BE CHANGED A LOT MORE EASILY THAN OTHERS.** In the ninth century – so legend has it – a woman disguised herself as a priest so successfully and for so long that eventually she was made Pope. As far as I'm aware, nobody's used the same method to attain the rank of corporate CEO – though business remains a predominantly male environment.

■ **YOU DON'T ALWAYS KNOW WHERE THE OTHER PERSON'S COMING FROM.** How you come across to another person depends not only on how you present yourself, but on what the other person has been trained to value. Being fat, for instance, implies gluttony in one culture but prosperity in another. Being sixty years old, which the East takes as proof of wisdom and experience, is taken in some parts of the West to prove only that you're over the hill. The quality and style of your clothing will suggest how much (or how little) money you earn. At the same time it will send out subtler messages to do with your professional affiliation, your personal taste and your regard or disregard for certain accepted dress codes.

■ **CULTURAL RULES ARE ALWAYS CHANGING**. Forty years ago in the United States it would have been acceptable to approach someone while smoking a cigarette; today it would appear offensive and inconsiderate of the other person's health. Conventions have changed in a similar way – though if anything more rapidly – with respect to hairstyles and cuts of collar on a man's shirt.

Amidst all this uncertainty, however, two secrets of self-presentation remain essential and unfailingly effective. So it's worth taking time to get them right.

The first is: *always expect the other person to like you*. I've never heard anyone express this idea better than Les Giblin, originator of the Clinic on Human Relations. He tells the story of a college roommate who always appeared more socially adept than Giblin managed to be:

> Finally, one day I got him to tell me his secret. 'You've got to believe the other fellow is going to like you,' he said. And as I watched him operate, I noticed that he always acted just as if the other fellow's friendly response was a foregone conclusion. Because he *believed* other people would like him, he *acted as if* they would like him. Another thing I noticed was this: Because he *was* thoroughly convinced that the other person would be friendly, he was not afraid of people. He was not on the defensive.[2]

Now this is classic self-motivation – and it's completely sound. We're tempted into defensiveness because we fear rejection. We go into an encounter thinking, 'This person won't like me,' or, 'This person will look down on me.' What we forget is that other people have exactly the same fear. By being defensive ourselves we actually trigger a defensive reaction in them, which we then interpret as aloofness, aggression or hostility. In this way, low expectations become a self-fulfilling prophecy – by anticipating rejection from others we send out the signals most likely to make it happen.

The world-famous singer Gertrude Lawrence said that before each performance she paused to reflect on the fact that the audience loved her. They didn't have to pay money or set aside time in their weekly routine to hear her; they did it because they wanted to. Thus concluding that the audience genuinely loved her, she said to herself, 'I must give them my best.' And she did. After which they proved their love by their response and by her ever-increasing popularity.

Conversely, I have long been convinced of a universal law that we attract to ourselves those people and conditions compatible with our state of mind. Men, for example, are particularly prone to fear of rejection, which is why first encounters between men sometimes lapse into defensive stalemates. The trick, of course, lies in approaching the encounter in the full expectation that the other person will respond well. This works almost every time. Go into an encounter telling yourself that the other person will be friendly, and nine times out of ten they will be. All that's needed is for someone to take the initiative.

The second secret of self-presentation is simply to *appreciate the person you're meeting*. There's nobody else in the world quite like the one you're about to meet. He or she is unique, with a blend of personality and experience you will never find duplicated elsewhere. And this person has entrusted him- or herself to you for the duration of your meeting. It's polite – in fact it's almost a duty – to make sure you look after them well.

Develop the habit of appreciating people. This habit makes it easy for you to smile. Smiling may not be the most complex management technique, yet an infectious smile exerts a powerful influence on business relationships. People who smile easily seem more likeable. This helps in the conduct of more effective business transactions. Smiling can have downsides too. Some smile routinely to camouflage nervousness, to disguise deceit, to tease, and to belittle and deride. A person you're meeting for the first time, though, will seldom interpret a smile in this way. Smiling sends out three positive messages:

▪ That you are well-disposed toward the other person.
▪ That you anticipate your goodwill will be reciprocated.
▪ That you think the other person is worth your attention.

If a warm smile isn't one of your natural assets, then a third secret of self-presentation is simply *practice*. Don't be ashamed of preparing in advance. Many of the things we say in the course of conducting business – especially at first encounters – we have said over and over again. So you might as well perfect them. There's nothing particularly virtuous about being unprepared. A greeting or conversation isn't *better* just because nobody's taken time beforehand to think through what they want to say or how best they might say it. Almost the opposite. If you prepare carefully, there's every chance that your interaction with another person will be more enlightening, more memorable and more witty than it would otherwise have been. Personally, I cannot think of any major first-time approach where I didn't work out in detail what I planned to do – and then pre-played the whole thing. It's amazing how many fidgets, weak gestures, flat phrases and blank expressions you can catch just by doing a few dry-runs in front of a mirror and a tape recorder.

And finally – that first line

Every first meeting is different. You may be meeting a contact at the airport. You may be socializing at a party. A friend may be introducing you to a potential business partner. You may be starting a job interview, or approaching the reception desk at a hotel. Each situation, and each individual, requires special treatment. Yet in almost every case, the function of the first line remains the same: to 'set the tone' of the interaction that follows.

Typically the opening seconds of your encounter should include most or all of the following:

■ **AN APPROPRIATE GESTURE OF GREETING**. Not all introductions need this. In general, though, a brief, firm handshake is now an almost universal standard for business, even in countries like Japan where greetings between nationals would normally involve a bow. Try not to treat bellhops and check-in personnel as your social inferiors. They aren't, and failing to treat them with politeness and good humor not only reflects badly on you but also makes it less likely they'll go out of their way to help you. Not long ago the manager of a major hotel accommodated me in the establishment's finest suite. Nonplussed, I asked to what I owed the honor. It turned out that twenty years earlier I'd taken the trouble to be friendly to him when he was delivering my cases as a hotel porter. It made a lasting impression.

■ **UP-FRONT AFFIRMATION**. 'Hello, how are you?' may be polite, but it doesn't zing. Always strive to give a sincere impression of concern and esteem. 'Hello, it's great to see you' has impact (so long as you use the right tone of voice), as does 'Hello, I'm so pleased you made time for this meeting.' When dealing with hotel and airline staff, dispense with the personal note but inject real feeling into your 'Good morning.' In my experience, about one customer in twenty rouses himself to do this. Believe me, it makes a difference.

■ **A DISCLOSURE OF YOUR IDENTITY AND ROLE**. This is necessary only if the other person doesn't know who you are. 'I'm John White, Mr. Rogers' PA. Mr. Rogers apologizes that he has a meeting, and asked if I'd take you to your hotel.' Or, in a different situation, 'John Buchov – I'm a partner here in DBVM,' or, 'Good afternoon, I'm Michael Chesney, I have three seats booked on this flight.' These are essential details. Supplying them puts the other person at ease; failing to supply them prompts an awkward question and can lead to misunderstanding.

■ **USING THE OTHER PERSON'S NAME.** Encounters frequently start with an exchange of names, which just as frequently get forgotten half a minute later. If the other person's name is new to you, repeat it back as soon as it's given. This will ensure you've heard it correctly, and give you a fighting chance of remembering it next day.

■ **REACHING OF A POINT OF CONTACT.** First lines need to trip forward into conversation. So always have follow-ups ready that identify – or at least look for – topics of shared concern. Most people manage the obvious ones: 'How was your flight?' for example, or, 'Do you come from around here?' It pays, though, to do your homework by intelligently questioning mutual friends. Thus you might arrive at 'Sam tells me you're into sky-diving,' or, 'Dan was saying you and he were in Moscow together.' If all else fails, you can trail a few leads of your own for the other person to pick up. For instance: 'You know, last time I came here they'd just begun the winter festival. I remember, because the golf course was booked solid for a week.' Those are two sentences, but four leads: a previous visit, an unusual event, a sporting interest, and the miserable experience of being unable to do what you'd planned.

Summary and action plan

The maverick Czechoslovakian businessman turned British politician, Robert Maxwell, occasionally attended government receptions for foreign delegations. Though tireless and tenacious in business, he was not famous for discretion. On one occasion, as he strolled from group to group, changing languages to crack jokes, he arrived in front of Richard Marsh, then the UK's Minister for Power, and Sir Robert Marshall, the Deputy Permanent Secretary at the Ministry:

> 'I hear that you speak German,' began Maxwell.
> 'Yes,' replied Marshall.
> 'Any other languages?'
> 'French.'
> 'It is extraordinary', replied Maxwell, 'how you educated people can only speak two foreign languages. I speak eleven.'[3]

This kind of brashness, so typical of Maxwell, represents almost the direct opposite of first-line focus. Maxwell knew how to make an entrance; but he seemed to have little time for the courtesies on which strong business relationships are built. His interactions with others appeared to carry an implicit demand that they recognize his brilliance and admire him for it. He was a man of remarkable energy and achievements. The problem is that energy and achievement can easily intimidate. Not surprisingly, Maxwell's biographer chose to dub him 'the Outsider.'

By contrast, first-line focus stresses an awareness of other people and their needs. The aim is not to dazzle, but to draw in. The premise behind it can be summarized in three statements:

▪ That people meet us with certain pre-formed expectations.
▪ That these expectations are formed largely on the basis of preliminary contact through indirect media and instantaneous first impression.
▪ That to a considerable extent we decide the future course of the relationship by how we handle these opening interactions.

A checklist for improving your first-line focus includes the following:

1 Where meetings with new people are arranged in advance, make sure you brief yourself properly.
2 Develop a way of screening your first-time calls to ensure that they are appropriate and properly executed.
3 Ensure that written communication goes out only when necessary, using the appropriate medium and the correct form, length and style.
4 Review your approach to first-time meetings – examining the nonverbal signals you send and how they are likely to be interpreted and received.
5 Ensure that you go into first-time meetings with the right attitude. Expect the other person to like you, appreciate the other person, and practice your approaches so that you come across in the way you intend.

Notes

[1] Harold Geneen with Alvin Moscow, *Managing* (New York: Doubleday, 1984), p.62.
[2] Les Giblin, *How to Have Confidence and Power in Dealing with People* (Englewood Cliffs: Prentice Hall, 1964), p.71.
[3] Tom Bower, *Maxwell: The Outsider* (London: Aurum Press, 1988), pp.106–7.

CHAPTER 4

Globalism

What is globalism?

Increasingly, the opening up of global markets demands that businesspeople not only relate well, but relate well *cross-culturally*.

Figures show considerable room for improvement. It's estimated, for example, that between 15 and 40 per cent of all US managers sent to overseas operations return prematurely, having failed to negotiate cultural barriers. As Western corporations have awakened to this problem – rather belatedly, it has to be said – two tendencies have emerged.

On the one hand, executives who like to style themselves 'global citizens' often downplay the problem. In this view, cultural differences are leveling out under the steamroller influence of Westernization. Air travel, automobiles, advertising, hotels, tourism, high-rise architecture, business suits, attaché cases, methods of accountancy – these things signify a new global order of which Western business practices are an integral part. Americans seem particularly eager about this, and particularly unaware that it reduces other cultures to the position of laggards and catchers-up. 'We insist that every one else do things our way,' the social scientist Edward T. Hall once wrote. 'Consequently we manage to convey the impression that we simply regard foreign nationals as 'underdeveloped Americans."'[1]

On the other hand, most major business schools now offer

modules on cultural acclimatization – often geared to particular national cultures. And since the mid-1980s a significant sub-genre of books has appeared, concentrating on the 'do's and taboos' of business travel. To the extent that it cultivates an awareness of cultural variation this development has done much good. But it has the weakness of directing attention to things that, while interesting, are of dubious value in conducting good business. Despite what the manuals say, there really is very little chance of offending an Englishman by wearing something that looks like a regimental tie; and although the Japanese bow has attracted a good deal of analysis in the West, most Japanese executives greet Westerners quite comfortably with a shake of the hand.

Identify the constants

As always, reality lies between the extremes. As cable and satellite communication tighten their grip on the globe, cultural practices quickly adjust and adapt. Having circled the globe 84 times as of this writing I can say from experience that many aspects of business have become increasingly standardized. Go to most major cities and you will find businessmen in suits, going to meetings presided over by a chairperson, staying at Western-style air-conditioned hotels, and advancing their skills through management training.

Yet this hasn't produced an overall and worldwide 'Western business culture.' In 1993, management gurus Charles Hampden-Turner and Fons Trompenaars could still identify seven different kinds of capitalist economy.[2] And at the level of personal behavior, national cultures show few signs of melting together, even within the West – one classic study showing that European managers working for American multinationals became, not more American in their values and behaviors, but more intensely British, French and German.[3] It is striking, for example, that many of the comments made in 1965 by the then president of the Locktite Corporation, E. Russell Eggers, about

BOX 1: One executive's guide to doing business with the French

1 Where the American tries to think in a straight line, the Frenchman insists on thinking in a circle.

2 A French businessman mistrusts the very things in which an American businessman has the most confidence.

3 An American executive tends to forget what he's said in a letter. A Frenchman never forgets what he's purposely left out.

4 An American will probably have lost his typical enthusiasm for a project before a Frenchman gets over his typical reservations.

5 A French company prepares its balance sheet and profit-and-loss statement not to show its stock-holders how much money it has made, but to show the tax authorities how little.

6 A Frenchman's thoughts are packaged in small and more specific sizes than an American's.

7 To a Frenchman, economic prosperity is a series of non-durable pleasures of lasting value. To an American, prosperity is a tangible product with constant model changes.

8 A Frenchman feels as ill at ease with anything mechanical as an American does with a domestic servant.

9 An American businessman treats his company like a wife: a Frenchman treats each of his companies like a mistress.

10 The word 'immoral' in English refers to what people do; in French it can apply to what companies do.

11 When a Frenchman is polite he is very, very polite and when he is rude he is very, very French.

12 To the Frenchman a business career is usually a means to an end. To an American it is often an end in itself.

Adapted from E. Russell Eggers, 'How to do business with a Frenchman', *Harper's Magazine*, August 1965. Reproduced by permission.

doing business with the French, would still resonate with Americans today (see Box 1, p.65).

If value-conflicts and misunderstandings can arise in cultures as apparently similar as the American and the French, the situation worldwide is likely to be a good deal worse. I recently conducted a survey of Haggai Institute's 33,000 alumni to see how well business people communicated across cultural boundaries, particularly in the developing world. International research of this nature is notoriously problematic, and I am not claiming statistical significance for the results.[4] Nevertheless, as a snapshot of current opinion among non-Western business leaders the outcome is revealing. Five hundred questionnaires were sent out, to which slightly less than half the contacts replied (242), representing 49 different countries, predominantly in Asia and Africa, but also Latin America and the Caribbean. All had a direct link with business, and all but three had been involved in trading across international borders.

How Western business looks from the other side

The survey presented a paradox. Predictably, perhaps, the majority of respondents (over 84%) saw 'trusting relationships' as a 'very important' precondition for business. Yet it was precisely the *failure* to establish trust in international business relationships that made the conduct of business with Westerners so difficult. A full breakdown of answers is given in Table 1 and Figure 1.

**TABLE 1: 35 reasons given for difficulty
in managing cross-cultural relationships**

Sources of difficulty cited:	Frequency:	As % of total:
CULTURAL AND LINGUISTIC		
Differences in culture, values and education	51	
Differences in language	33	
Misunderstandings over customs and etiquette	30	
Deep religious differences	2	
History of tension between peoples	2	
TOTAL	**118**	**30.1**
TRUST-RELATED		
Can't rely on Westerners' integrity and commitment	59	
West too remote for trust to develop	26	
Westerner breaks financial commitments	10	
Westerner unwilling to trust	9	
Home country has bad reputation abroad	3	
Westerner unwilling to extend credit or invest	2	
Lack of go-betweens	1	
TOTAL	**110**	**28.1**
PARITY AND FAIRNESS		
Westerner prejudiced or unwilling to understand home culture	26	
Westerner refuses do deal on the basis of mutuality or partnership	20	
Westerner's attitude is short-term, selfish or exploitative	13	

Sources of difficulty cited:	*Frequency:*	*As % of total:*
Westerner overlooks home country's interests	9	
Westerner cannot be held accountable	3	
Westerner imposes tough business conditions	2	
Westerner supplies poor quality products	1	
No parity in negotiation	1	
TOTAL	**75**	**19.1**

CONDITIONS IN HOME COUNTRY

Legal and regulatory frameworks complex, obstructive or unpredictable	13	
Economic instability disrupts exchange and discourages investment	12	
Poor transport/communications infrastructure	9	
Corruption and official interference	7	
Lack of capital	5	
General production problems	2	
Political instability	2	
Adverse physical conditions	2	
Work permits hard to obtain for incomers	1	
Security problems	1	
Differing production standards	1	
Lack of a vehicle	1	
TOTAL	**56**	**14.3**

INFORMATION DEFICIT

Sources of difficulty cited:	*Frequency:*	*As % of total:*
Westerner is ignorant of production conditions in home country	17	
Lack of Western contacts and information on Western markets	11	
General communication problems	4	
Westerner lacks knowledge of local management styles	1	
TOTAL	**33**	**8.4**

Total no. of reasons cited = 392
Total no. of replies = 242

Many respondents cited more than one source of difficulty, so the total number of replies (392) was greater than the total number of respondents. Misunderstandings based on differences of language and culture formed the single largest category of complaints (over 30%). Likewise almost a quarter of respondents (23%) drew attention to adverse conditions in their own country. This list covers the generally accepted facts about climate, infrastructure and economy that respondents identify as a disincentive to foreign business involvement – fluctuations in currency value, inadequate transport and communications infrastructure, political instability and over-complex legal regulations governing overseas trade.

FIGURE 1: What respondents saw as problems in overseas business relationships

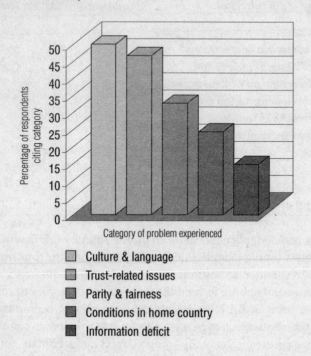

Category of problem experienced

☐ Culture & language
☐ Trust-related issues
☐ Parity & fairness
☐ Conditions in home country
☐ Information deficit

Far more difficulties arose, however, not from circumstances but from the *attitude* taken by the financially stronger partner. Pulling the strands together, it appears that Westerners doing business overseas failed in at least three respects:

■ **UNWILLINGNESS TO BRIDGE THE CULTURE GAP.** 49 per cent of all respondents refer to divisions of culture and language. But it's interesting that in many cases they feel the onus lies on *them* to bridge the gap. Typically they will be expected to use the language of the visitors, not the other way around. Some of them talk about the frustration of not being sure that they are making themselves clear, others speak of uncertainty as to

what they have agreed to when they finally reach a deal.
A similar reversal of positions occurs over protocol and
etiquette, so that Ben Parco of the United Arab Emirates can
complain, not of foreigners who flout his own country's
customs, but of his own difficulty in knowing 'how to
understand and relate myself to their customs, business
traditions and manners.' As Tito Musyoka of Kenya
comments, this is particularly ironic in the case of Western
managers who have become semi-permanent residents in
Africa. 'They lack knowledge of my people's customs, beliefs,
needs and values,' he says. 'Most of them find it difficult to
integrate with locals. They continue living like foreigners in
every aspect of their lives.'

■ **INTELLECTUAL ARROGANCE.** Even in the way they conduct their
business, Westerners abroad all too often fail to value or take
account of local culture. They don't seem to understand, says
Simon Bandah of Zimbabwe, 'how their business operations
will relate to local economic, political and social needs ... very
often foreign nationals want to operate as if in first world
conditions.' George Nyeko of Uganda adds, 'They like to
import wholesale their own ways of doing things. They like
imposing themselves and their ideas.' India's Thomas
Swaroop identifies this as the 'culture of dominance.' In
Malaysia, Sam Abishegam of Abishegam Holdings talks about
the 'fear of being talked down to by Americans, who sometimes think they have all the answers,' while Frits Frijmersum
from Surinam notes that 'Americans have difficulty in taking
us seriously (only 400,000 people). The Dutch often know us
well, but are more likely to interfere too much in our private,
business or state affairs.'

■ **EXPLOITATION OF THE WEAKER PARTNER.** Dealing across the
Western/non-Western divide tends to result in the stronger
party dictating terms. 'To establish business relationships
with people from the first world,' says Klaus Rempel of Brazil,

'You have to be very flexible, attending all the demands and most of the business conditions. Without this, Third World business cannot survive.' This goes a lot further than the imposition of reasonable market disciplines. Another Brazilian, José Baptista Mendoça, draws attention to 'the absence of ethical standards in their deals – the "buccaneer syndrome" by which one endeavors to get rich at the earliest hour without any qualms for the long-term fall-out.' A dozen other respondents felt that the interest of Westerners they had known was at root short-term, selfish or exploitative. The single most frequent comment made across the board (by 24% of all respondents) was that Western business contacts were not dependable, and lacked integrity and commitment. 'It is extremely difficult,' says Benjamin Quinones, Jr., of the Philippines, 'to do business with people who are not honest and whose words cannot be trusted. I found this to be true in my dealings with various nationals – Germans, Americans, Japanese, Thais, Koreans and Chinese. In business you look for partners you can trust, who you can depend on.' Victor Basil Theodore of Madras, India, is one of many who have been the victims of Western bad practice: 'Normally orders are placed and not honored after execution, for weak reasons. American business people are not interested in having long, steady relations in business, and change the business relations for a few cents difference in price ... to be crude, they are cut-throats. I write this out of experience.'

This is not a wholesale condemnation of international Western business – there is good practice as well as bad. Nor are Western companies the only ones to operate overseas as 'dominant partners.' Nevertheless a clear problem remains. International business forces people to communicate across barriers of culture. It also forces them to deal – for the most part – with others they hardly know. And in many of the connections formed the financial clout lies predominantly on one side. Sensitivity to all three issues is fundamental to the social skill of globalism.

Ways to apply globalism

Understand how cultures differ

Even in an age of rapid information transfer and high population mobility, nations retain distinctive cultures. Literally and metaphorically, therefore, knowing 'where someone is coming from' is the first step to achieving mutual understanding and establishing a good working relationship.

Various attempts have been made to find a scale, or group of scales, on which cultures can be measured and compared. One of the most successful remains that of Geert Hofstede, a Dutchman working in the psychology of management. As the only researcher to have completed a large-scale transnational study of the impact of culture on management style, his impact on both the theory and practice of international management has been enormous.

In 1967 and 1973 a high-tech multinational which Hofstede dubs the HERMES corporation conducted wide-ranging morale surveys of its workforce. At the time HERMES manufactured in 13 countries and sold in more than a hundred. The personnel in its various departments and subsidiaries were almost all indigenous, and the surveys finally yielded a staggering 117,000 responses from 50 countries and three culture-regions. The surveys had been commissioned for internal purposes; Hofstede, however, used them to analyze cultural differences between the nations where HERMES operated.

He concluded that nations varied along four dimensions:

TABLE 2: How selected countries rank out of 53 on Hofstede's four dimensions of cultural difference

Country	Power Distance	Uncertainty/ Avoidance	Individualism	Masculinity
Australia	41	37	2	16
Canada	39	41	4	24
Denmark	51	51	9	50
France	15	12	10	35
West Germany	43	29	15	9
Great Britain	43	47	3	9
Indonesia	8	41	47	30
Italy	34	23	7	4
Japan	33	7	22	1
Korea	27	16	44	41
Malaysia	1	46	36	25
Sweden	47	49	10	53
United States	38	43	1	15
Venezuela	5	21	50	3

■ **POWER DISTANCE** – How far life in an organization is dominated by inequality, pecking orders and hierarchies.
■ **UNCERTAINTY AVOIDANCE** – How far people try to reduce ambiguity and uncertainty by sticking to formal rules.
■ **INDIVIDUALISM** – How far people think in terms of individual freedom and responsibility as opposed to what is best for, and demanded by, the wider group.
■ **MASCULINITY** – How far people value personal advancement, money and goods as opposed to quality of social environment.

By the end of his study, Hofstede was able to construct a rank-order of nations for each of the four dimensions (see Table 2). Each nation thus has a distinct profile. Britain is strongly individualistic (rank 3) and masculine (rank 9), but scores low on power distance (rank 43) and uncertainty avoidance (rank 47). Sweden shows a similar profile, but with a stronger tradition of protecting home life from the encroachment of work, scores lower on masculinity (rank 53). By contrast, Japan is strongly masculine (rank 1) and also shows a preference for uncertainty avoidance (rank 7). Consequently, where Japanese 'quality circles' aim to perfect performance and product (a masculine concept, in Hofstede's terms), the apparently similar 'work groups' at Sweden's Volvo factories seek to enhance job satisfaction – a very non-masculine concept.

By far the most influential and widely known distinction made by Hofstede is the one between *individualist* societies and *collective* ones. Presented with Hofstede's key question 'How important is it to you to have freedom to adapt your own approach to the job?' business people in the individualistic societies of Western Europe and North America tend to answer, 'Very important.' Their counterparts in collectivist societies (mainly in Latin America and South-East Asia) tend to answer the exact opposite. Business thrives in both kinds of culture. But it adopts different forms, and people on different sides of the divide make different assumptions and behave in different ways.

A recent study of Italy showed that this applied even in the trading of insults. Northern Italians, being more cosmopolitan, will insult the individual directly ('You are stupid' or 'You are a cretin'), whereas the more traditional southern Italians will direct the insult at the individual's social group ('I wish a cancer on you and all your relatives' or 'Your sister is a cow').[5] A comparable division of thinking can be found in business. Table 3, based on Hofstede's research, indicates some of the main ways in which practices and expectations diverge.[6]

TABLE 3: Business differences between collectivist and individualist cultures

Collectivist cultures:	*Individualist cultures:*
Primary sense of moral obligation to the company	Primary sense of moral obligation to self and close family
Employees expect company to look after them like a family	Employees see company as source of income and job satisfaction
Employees expect company to defend their interests	Employees expect to look after their own interests
Promotion from inside, based on seniority	Promotion from inside and outside, based on market value
Little concern for fashion in management ideas	Managers try out and tend to endorse modern management ideas
Company policies and practices vary according to particular relationships	Company policy and practices apply to all
Stress on group decision-making	Stress on individual decision-making
Emphasis on belonging and membership	Emphasis on initiative, achievement and leadership
Company has strong influence on private life and opinions	Individual has a right to private life and own opinion

Beware the stereotype

This kind of generalization can only be taken so far. People do business with people, not with cultures, and there is no such thing as a typical German or Chinese any more than there is a typical Briton or American. So any notion of a cultural 'type' must be treated with caution. Working with the Institut Européen d'Administration des Affaires and London Business School, Indrei Ratiu found that managers ranked 'most internationally effective' by their colleagues altered their stereotypes to fit the actual people they met.[7] By contrast, managers ranked 'least internationally effective' continued to apply stereotypes even when their experience showed the stereotypes to be inaccurate.

It's also crucial to recognize that cultures have a lot in common with animal species – they've developed certain characteristics as a response to surrounding conditions. City folk often make fun of the slow commercial pace of small-town shops. Yet dallying over a sale to chat to the customer makes perfect sense in the context of a small community; it only becomes 'inappropriate,' 'unproductive' or 'wrong' when displaced into the culture of the big city.

A recent cultural initiative by the international chemical giant ICI brought together managers from Britain and Italy. Though the Italians spoke English, up to that point both sides had found communication difficult and frustrating. With the help of consultants, they undertook an exercise called 'Project Management in a Multi-Cultural Environment.' This involved an open sharing of the way each side viewed the other, with revealing results. According to the British, Italian managers were:

■ Resourceful improvisers.
■ Able to adapt to and create new rules.
■ Not very time-conscious.
■ Poor at meeting deadlines.
■ Undisciplined.
■ Emotional.
■ Planning-averse.
■ More focused on building relationships than establishing procedures.

By contrast, the Italian managers saw their British counterparts as:

■ Preoccupied with rules and procedures.
■ Well-organized and analytical.

▌ Averse to innovation and change.

▌ Slow and ponderous.

▌ Disciplined.

▌ Good at planning.

▌ Not emotionally forthcoming.

▌ More focused on establishing procedures than building relationships.

In passing, it is notable that this conflict of approaches could not be predicted from Hofstede's scoring as shown in Table 3. The British were perceived as rule-bound, yet they ranked lower than the Italians in Uncertainty Avoidance (47th, to the Italians' 23rd). They focused on tasks rather than relationships, and yet in Hofstede's dimensions emerge as marginally *less* masculine (9th, to the Italians' 4th). Particular individuals or teams don't always match up to their national stereotypes – and those stereotypes are themselves in a state of flux.

Commenting on the differences, though, researcher Lisa Hoecklin makes the following comment:

> In the process of making explicit their perceptions about each other, the teams recognized that both cultures' behaviors were perfectly legitimate and professional in their respective environments. In fact, the perceptions of each other were precisely those things that made each successful in their own environment ... Both groups of managers recognized that neither culture was right or wrong. They simply used the opposite starting points of the same logic.[8]

In view of this, the teams made a decision. Instead of regarding themselves as incompatible, they deliberately worked out ways of integrating their respective strengths in the context of management. They chose to value each other's strengths. And they broke down joint projects so as to identify which parts would respond best to which style of management. A year later they were successfully completing the first phase of a key project.

Cultural difference may present problems; but it also provides opportunities. In overview, some of the most important points to remember seem to be these:

■ **FILL IN THE BACKGROUND.** Cultures are self-consistent – in other words, if someone from another culture acts in a way you think dissatisfactory or strange, there's nearly always a reason for it. If a Middle Eastern contractor tells you a construction project will be completed *En shah allah* (literally, 'If God is willing') this should not be taken as breach of contract. To the Islamic mind, everything happens by the will of God, and it is customary to acknowledge this even in the conduct of business.

■ **DON'T FIX PROBLEMS WITH A WESTERN TOOLKIT.** In August 1990 the *Wall Street Journal* reported the case of a large American electrical company that acquired a French subsidiary. First-year performance was dismal, and blamed partly on a poorly motivated sales and marketing staff. The solution? The American parent company laid on a high-tech motivation road-show, complete with company slogan T-shirts which participants were expected to wear during a three-day event in Paris. Unfortunately the French employees saw it all as vulgar hype. Results in the next two quarters were worse than ever.

■ **NAME CULTURAL DIVERSITY AS AN ASSET, NOT AS A PROBLEM.** Cultural barriers always present a challenge. But that doesn't mean that outcomes – either in negotiation or management – must be worse. The range of experience and perspective in multi-cultural teams, for example, gives them enormous productive potential – so long as that potential is realized through mutual respect and a determination to understand another person's point of view.

■ **DON'T EXPECT CHANGE OVERNIGHT.** Some business situations require people to make cultural changes. National firms have to adapt to the fresh demands of a global market; new subsidiaries have to adapt to the culture of the new parent corporation. In management you may find yourself presiding over such processes and ensuring that everyone catches the wave. Remember, though, that change driven from the outside can impact as a face-threat, producing resentment and inflexibility. First observe. Then re-evaluate, asking yourself if the ideas you are proposing make sense in the cultural context and from the other person's point of view. Finally, if you still want to introduce changes, do it in gradual steps.

The social scientist Edward T. Hall highlights the case of a US-based multinational with subsidiaries in Latin America. The American board had foreseen the difficulties of having the Latin American operation run by US middle-managers, and was actively seeking to advance nationals to higher levels of management. But here they ran into a cultural problem. Latin American culture, with its tendency to high power distance, produces a built-in hesitancy about speaking up to superiors, and a reluctance to take the initiative and accept responsibility.

One manager, though, had circumvented the problem. First, he brushed up on his Spanish. Second, he encouraged informal contacts between himself and the prospective managers, in particular by getting local and US management of all levels to mix freely at social events to which their wives also came. Third, he made a habit of walking around the factory floor chatting and cracking jokes – thus overturning the traditional image of the manager as authoritarian and aloof. Fourth, he developed a pattern of overlapping three-level meetings (levels A, B, C; levels B, C, D; levels C, D, E, and so on), making sure that the American management chief set a pattern of encouraging subordinates to challenge his ideas. When the Latin general foremen at the top-level meeting saw how the North American managers stated their objections to the boss, they cautiously began to follow suit. It took a long time and some gentle handling, but gradually a sense of independence and self-confidence began to filter down the management structure until it suffused the whole workforce.[9]

Be aware of communication style

We're used to thinking of language as something that binds us together. This is only partly true. As David and Terpstra said in a ground-breaking book on international business,[10] 'A language is not a universal means of communication. Rather it is a means of communication *within a particular culture* ... The picture of the universe shifts from tongue to tongue.'

This is a problem for international business because business depends on communication working well. Virtually all communication is language-based, so every 'border' between two languages presents a potential communication problem.

Multinationals, of course, often have such borders running straight through the middle of them, making culture an internal management issue. Just how confusing that can be was illustrated recently by Lotus, who attempted to articulate a set of central company values, but framed them in Western language and concepts. The first value – 'commit to excellence' – was meant to define a preferred attitude to product and service. French employees, though, took it to mean 'get the best out of yourself.' And the eleventh value – 'Have fun!' – though heart-warming to Americans, seemed to the Dutch an unwarranted intrusion on their privacy.

Nor do terms translated into another language necessarily take their meanings with them. You'd think an idea like *achievement* was almost universal – in other words, that the act of achieving would be recognized in almost every culture, and signified only with a different word. But this is not the case; several modern languages, including French, have no adequate equivalent for the word. Likewise, no word in Japanese captures the meaning of our term *decision-making*. This does not mean the French lack ambition or the Japanese constantly change their minds. But it should alert us to the fact that in crossing cultural borders we not only encounter a different language but enter a new 'behavioral domain.' In some small but key details, people act and think in ways we do not. So, for instance, while Western executives are used to weighing commercial outcomes and then choosing Option A over Option B, Japanese executives characteristically take more factors into account, and reach decisions jointly and by consensus.

Remember also that language itself can be either *task-oriented* or *person-oriented*. Being predominantly task-oriented, Westerners pride themselves on being open, frank and explicit – on 'getting to the point' and 'not beating around the bush.' Implied in this is the idea that the relation between two business people – and by extension their pride, status and sensibilities – matter less than the business they're discussing. For that reason, they can find negotiation in the East frustrating. Easterners appear 'inscrutable' and 'won't give a straight answer.' Typical is the reluctance of the Japanese to come out with a firm 'no.' Almost always a Japanese will prefer some form of circumlocution – 'Yes, but ... ' 'Why do you ask me that?' 'I will do my best,' 'There may be difficulties,' 'I must check with my co-workers,' 'I am very sorry.' It sounds evasive. In fact, though, like most collectivist cultures, the Japanese simply take a person-oriented approach. The priority is not to disturb harmony in the relationship by causing loss of face. One Japanese business person using these circumlocutions to another is perfectly well understood to mean 'no.' Only Westerners, with their habit of bluntness, fail to take the hint.

One implication of this is clear: don't expect anyone in a people-oriented culture to give you raw feedback. In the West we are taught to give feedback in precise terms, verbally and on-demand. It is possible – within certain bounds – to criticize others without breaking codes of politeness. People-oriented cultures shy away from this. Feedback, if it comes at all, will likely be delayed, vague, impersonal and nonverbal.

Finally, it's worth bearing in mind that some people-oriented cultures routinely use overstatement. A good example is the Arabic practice of *mubalaqha*, in which exaggeration supplies some indication of the speaker's strength of feeling about an issue. This isn't so very different from the way an American might say he is 'dying for something to eat.' Applied to business dealing it should not be construed as an attempt to deceive, only as a way of underlining a point. For an Arab to stick modestly to the facts could make the matter appear insignificant, or imply that the situation is actually the reverse of what is stated.

Know how to help non-English speakers

Given these subtleties, there is much to be said for doing language training before a long-term posting abroad, or using the services of an interpreter. In a sense the situation is worse when a Westerner has dealings with someone who knows English as a second language, because both sides will be tempted to 'muddle through.' This happens a lot, and in the majority of cases it's the non-Westerner who has to use his or her acquired language. Almost always this leads to confusion. Misunderstandings will bounce back on both parties, and so it's worth making the effort to push the 'language window' as far open as it will go. For example:

- **MAKE YOUR SPEECH EASY TO UNDERSTAND**. Use simple words and avoid colloquialisms and jargon. For instance, 'I decided' is preferable to 'I came to the conclusion.' Don't race, because someone who's struggling to follow you will need time to keep track. Keep your sentences short enough that the listener can't get lost in them, and wherever possible use active verbs, not passive – they require less decoding.

- **REINFORCE VISUALLY**. People communicating across language borders naturally resort to gestures. Make liberal use of them. Remember that in some situations you may be able to make yourself clear by taking out a scratch pad and illustrating.

■ **MONITOR THE OTHER PERSON'S UNDERSTANDING.** You can often tell if the other person has understood you by listening to his or her responses. A sudden lurch sideways in a conversation often indicates a misunderstanding. Remember that people often say 'Yes' and nod even if they have no idea what you've said, so in management situations particularly it's advisable to use an occasional 'reality-check' by asking the other person to repeat back to you what they think you're saying. It's acceptable to ask, 'Do you understand what I mean?' and to rephrase it if the other person looks unsure. When in doubt, assume that you have failed to get your point across.

■ **ALLOW TIME.** Following a conversation in your second language is tough. So pause frequently when you speak. Don't hurry to fill silences – the other person may be using them to finish a mental translation. Also bear in mind (this is frequently forgotten) that people who speak English as a second language aren't stupid, nor are they deaf.

■ **DON'T FORGET YOUR FACEWORK.** Communication across a language barrier will almost always lead to miscues, flubs and misunderstandings. Since the other person's self-esteem is partly bound up in the success of their effort to understand you, make sure you don't embarrass them, or imply that failures in communication are their fault. And do a lot of smiling.

Let relationships grow

Chinese expatriates – of whom there are millions along the Pacific Rim – have traditionally conducted business through the *guanxi*. There is no exact English equivalent for this word. It means something like 'web of relationships' and defines a mainly ethnic network between whose members there exist bonds of trust, loyalty and accountability – mutual connections that provide a secure basis for business.

A number of large South-East Asian companies are rooted in the *guanxi*. The Bangkok Bank, for instance, one of the largest in the region, was begun by a Chinese rice trader called Chin Sophonpanich, who began by lending only to other ethnic Chinese. The regional network he built up now includes two of the region's most powerful businessmen, Robert Kuok and Liem Sioe Long. Robert Kuok's businesses include sugar and commodities trading, as well as the *South China Morning Post* and the Shangri-La hotel chain. Liem Sioe Long founded the Salim group, manufacturing cement and noodles.

While such companies seem, from the outside, to be indistinguishable from their Western counterparts, they in fact operate very differently – a fact poorly understood by incoming multinationals. Westerners seeking a foothold in the region often conform to the Western Business Style in downplaying the importance of long-term business relationships. Yet the Chinese – in common with other collective and people-based cultures – require a certain depth and intensity of relationship to be in place before business can even be discussed.

Being able to forge such relationships is an essential skill in globalism. Without it, business partnerships tend to be plagued by misunderstanding and mistrust. This explains why some Americans doing business in Hong Kong have complained that local partners have their own agendas. They feel that Hong Kong business people are less interested in building up market share than investing in new, unrelated ventures, and too ready to associate with multiple Western business partners and thus to create conflicts of commercial interest.

The most successful Western partnerships with the Chinese recognize and respect the principle of social investment. An example is the Swire Group, a British-owned trading house based in Hong Kong, which recently partnered with CITIC Pacific in developing Festival Walk, a huge new shopping mall in Hong Kong, and in operating a number of Coca-Cola bottling plants on the Chinese mainland.[11] It's no accident that CITIC Pacific is run by the son of Rong Yiren, China's vice-premier, who for many years has had a business relationship with the Swire group.

I can attest from my own experience of leadership training in the People's Republic of China that productive relationships take years to build. I find that to be true in all people-oriented cultures. Even in the emerging task-driven global environment, business people working and traveling outside the West will usually find social investment both practiced and expected by prospective business partners. Westerners cannot be born into a network like the *guanxi*. They cannot buy their way in. But the network has a protocol for accepting new members – so long as they honor its traditions.

So if you're making new business contacts outside the West, be ready to adapt your style:

▪ **NEVER BE IMPATIENT.** Western businesspeople visiting Tokyo often find themselves asking how many sushis they'll have to munch through before the real talking starts. The answer is: as many as your host requires. Remember that in a people-oriented culture these apparently time-wasting preliminaries serve an essential function. Your host's culture dictates that he or she cannot start to do business with you until you can be regarded as a friend. Indeed to try to broach business matters before that point has been reached will seem premature and impolite.

▪ **GET THE DETAILS RIGHT.** Each national culture has unspoken rules governing relationship formation, which themselves are in a state of constant change. Business etiquette in Japan, for instance, lays much stress on the presentation of gifts, elaborate seating plans, and appropriate times at which to consume alcohol. Japanese and Korean etiquette both involve the visitor in a good deal of singing, requests for which must be graciously acceded to even if you have a voice like a crow. It is far beyond the scope of this book to detail all the nuances even for one country. Several good primers will be found on the bookshelves, and of course there's rarely any better preparation for doing business in another country than to talk to someone who's just been out there. No amount of research, though, will prepare you for every situation, so the best rule remains: *when in doubt, take your cue from your host.*

Check out your timing

A series of studies in the 1980s illustrated how cultures differ in their attitude to time. Comparing seven different countries, the researchers found that:

- In every country there was a high correlation between the accuracy of public clocks, the speed people walked in the street, and the speed at which post office clerks completed the sale of a small-denomination postage stamp.

- The 'speedier' countries included the US and Japan. The 'less speedy' countries included Indonesia, Brazil and Italy.

- In Brazil the person who always arrived late for appointments was rated more likeable, successful and happy than someone who arrived on time. In the US these traits were usually associated with people who arrived early.[12]

It seems that the 'monochronic' view of time native to Northern Europe and North America has gradually tightened its grip on the rest of the planet. In a monochronic view, time is seen as a limited resource and must be chopped up and allocated between competing priorities. Time has to be 'managed.' By contrast, people-oriented cultures have tended to take a more relaxed 'polychronic' view, the reason probably being that, when you expect to spend a good deal of your life in the same community, keeping relationships harmonious matters more than rushing to get a particular job finished on time. With the arrival of the global economy and media, the polychronic view is gradually losing ground. Nevertheless it's worth remembering that a different culture may still attach very different values to time and its use. Five key areas are:

■ **DISCUSSION**. In Anglo-American culture discussion is a means to, and the end of, doing a deal, and good business etiquette requires coming to the point quickly. Even social lunches have an implicit business rationale. In other nations, though, business transactions may themselves be more of a social event, and coming around too quickly to matters of price, delivery, payment and model of produce will be seen as 'hustling.'

■ **DETAIL**. The Western habit of settling the broad points of an agreement while leaving the details until later is, in part, a mutual courtesy and a sign of good faith. But it can equally well be seen as an attempt to out-maneuver a negotiating partner, which is why some cultures insist on discussing every last point before reaching a deal. It's worth being patient, since anxiety to conclude the deal may result in the settlement being less favorable to you. Indeed a Japanese CEO once remarked, with some truth, 'We have learned that if we make Americans wait long enough, they'll agree to anything.'

■ **APPOINTMENTS**.Westerners generally adhere to very precise schedules. Being made to wait fifteen minutes to see someone is thought to justify a polite reminder. Forty-five minutes occasions loud complaint. By contrast, the relaxed attitude of Latin cultures toward appointment times is legendary, and should not be taken as a slight. Reprimanding one culture using the norms of another is not only pointless, but counter-productive.

■ **ACQUAINTANCE**.In many cultures, and notably in the Chinese, goodwill and trust in a relationship are linked directly to the length of acquaintance. So much significance is attached to this because, in the absence of strong Western-style contract law, knowing someone for a long time is the best guarantee that he or she can be trusted. Again, the principle of social investment is crucial.

■ **DEADLINES**. Browbeating is not a reliable method of getting things done on time. If a project is urgent, and you suspect your business partner takes a relaxed attitude to completion dates, you should check this out at the beginning. You won't give offense by asking the question. You will give offense by making an uninformed commitment and then complaining afterwards – although discreet calls to inquire how things are going generally don't go amiss.

Summary and action plan

'The prognosis for effective communication across cultural lines is not good.' Thus the social psychologists Peter B. Smith and Michael Harris Bond sum up the problem facing those who have to deal with other cultures.[13] Yet the challenges of cross-cultural communication can be met and overcome with the right approach.

How companies fare in their business dealings across cultural borders depends, in the end, on how well their personnel can master the skills of globalism in relating to contacts of a different background. Globalism does not mean assuming that Western practices in business have become – or should become – the global norm. Many elements of business practice have indeed converged. But others are doing so only slowly, and some show no signs of doing it at all.

Part of the problem for Western business people is that in so much of the world they have found themselves in a dominant position and have been able to dictate terms. Consequently the impression has arisen in many countries that business partners from more developed countries – and particularly from the West – show insufficient sensitivity to cultural difference. They hesitate to take the initiative in breaking down cultural barriers. Rather they cling to the notion that Western business ideas are necessarily preferable and should, if necessary, be imposed.

In a world where new centers of economic power are emerging, such a blasé attitude to the problems of cross-cultural relating will tend to make Western businesses less competitive on world markets. For that reason, globalism has become an increasingly important aspect of business relating. The action plan for improving globalism includes the following:

1 Prioritize research on the cultural dimension of any new international business venture.
2 Ensure that information on the 'dos and taboos' of another culture are up-to-date and still relevant. Things change fast.
3 Be aware that many cultures outside those of the West give greater place to relationship-formation as a basis for business. Exercise patience, and be tolerant of practices that you might at first identify as thoughtless or rude.
4 Name cultural diversity as an asset, particularly when it exists within a corporation, office or team. Seek to exploit its potentials.
5 Pay particular attention to the way you communicate. Misunderstandings arise easily; minimize them by using translators or language training, and at all times aim for clarity by reinforcing messages and monitoring the other person's understanding.

Notes

[1] Edward T. Hall, *The Silent Language* (New York: Anchor Press, 1973). *op.cit.*, p.xiii.
[2] Charles Hampden-Turner and Fons Trompenaars, *The Seven Cultures of Capitalism* (New York: Doubleday, 1993).
[3] A. Laurent, 'The Cultural Diversity of Western Conceptions of Management'? *International Studies of Management and Organization* 13.1–2 (spring–summer 1983), pp.75–96.
[4] The survey was conducted in 1996, with the bulk of responses covering the area often described as the Third World – 46% of

responses coming from Africa, 40% from South and East Asia, 8% from Latin America and the Caribbean. Apart from the relatively small size of the sample, the main weakness arises from the non-random nature of the sample group. Since all the respondents are associated with Haggai Institute, and to some extent share its values, the results cannot be taken as fully representative of the wider business population. For instance, given that a working knowledge of English is a prerequisite for attendance at most Haggai Institute seminars, we might expect the respondents to underestimate the significance of language as a cultural barrier.

[5] See G.R. Semin and M. Rubini, 'Unfolding the Concept of Person by Verbal Abuse,' *European Journal of Social Psychology* 20 (1990), pp.463–74.

[6] Based on information in Lisa Hoecklin, *Managing Cultural Difference: Strategies for Competitive Advantage* (London: Addison-Wesley, 1995), p.36.

[7] See Indrei Ratiu, 'Thinking Internationally: A Comparison of How International Executives Learn,' *International Studies of Management and Organization* 13.1–2 (spring–summer 1983), pp.139–50.

[8] Hoecklin, *Managing Cultural Difference*, p.20.

[9] Edward T. Hall and William Foote Whyte, 'Intercultural Communication: A Guide to Men of Action,' *Human Organization* 19.5–12 (1960).

[10] K. H. David and V. Terpstra, *The Cultural Environment of International Business*, 2nd edition (Cincinnati: Southwestern Publishing Company, 1985), p. 18.

[11] See the *Economist*, 29 March 1997.

[12] Quoted by Peter B. Smith and Michael Harris Bond in *Social Psychology Across Cultures* (Hemel Hempstead: Harvester Wheatsheaf, 1993), pp.149–50.

[13] Peter B. Smith and Michael Harris Bond, *Social Psychology Across Cultures* (London: Prentice-Hall Europe, 1998), p.190.

CHAPTER 5

Motivating Power

What is motivating power?

Long before CNN went on the air, Ted Turner had to persuade the cable operators that this revolutionary idea was worth backing. To make them sign up he knew he needed more than big talk; he needed a media heavyweight for Washington Bureau Chief. He targeted Daniel Schorr.

Then sixty-two, the veteran CBS correspondent had been out of network television for three years. He was a controversial figure, widely regarded as too hot to handle by the network chiefs. But as a lifelong network man himself, he was suspicious of Turner and this radical idea of a cable news channel. Also, he was primarily committed to a correspondent's role, reporting and doing his own commentaries without taking responsibility for part of the organization. So when Turner's colleague, news executive Reese Schonfield, offered him the job of Washington Bureau Chief, Schorr hedged. In Douglas Ramsey's account:[1]

'I don't consider myself a very good administrator,' he told Schonfield. 'And there's nothing I hate more than signing other people's expense accounts.'

'All right,' Schonfield conceded. 'We'll call you chief correspondent.'

Again Schorr backed away. 'Really, Reese, I don't like the term "chief" at all. If it's all the same to you, just call me senior correspondent.'

Nevertheless Schorr agreed to meet Ted Turner in Las Vegas. Turner had set up the appointment, and with it a press conference at which he hoped to announce both CNN and Schorr's appointment as a senior correspondent. Schorr had misgivings, and Turner knew it.

'You're on record as anti-news,' Schorr charged. 'You put news on at three in the morning in Atlanta. Your anchorman once read the news with a picture of Walter Cronkite over his face. And now you're telling me you want to do serious news?'

Turner was unrepentant. He knew he needed Schorr, but he wasn't about to apologize. 'What I do on that channel has nothing to do with this,' he replied. 'That's there, this is here. Cable News Network will be a serious news operation. We're going first class.'

At least his convictions had been aired, Schorr thought, and Schonfield seemed convinced that Turner meant business and had the financial backing to deliver on his promise. In short order, he got down to what Turner wanted out of him. 'There are a few things I need to know,' Schorr continued. 'First, do you expect me to read commercials on the air?'

'No,' Turner answered flatly.

'What about mentioning sponsors of programs or teasing commercials?'

Again Turner replied with an emphatic no and continued, 'Listen. Let's make this easy. You ... write a contract that satisfies you. You put whatever you want in there and you've got it. How does that sound?'

Surprised at the speed with which Turner was willing to make a decision that would have taken months at any of the big networks, Schorr was impressed. 'I can hardly argue with that.'

By mid-afternoon they'd hammered out a draft agreement that included a clause allowing Schorr to refuse any assignment that conflicted with his personal standards or ethics. Schorr was given editorial *carte blanche*, a salary 10 per cent higher than he'd ever got at CBS, plus a retainer of 50 per cent for the next year leading up to CNN's launch, running alongside the living he earned from newspaper columns and radio commentaries. As Ramsey pointedly concludes, 'He had nothing to object to.'

Understand motivation

From a negotiating point of view, Ted Turner's bargain with Daniel Schorr was pretty soft. He 'gave it all away.' But this meeting wasn't about negotiation; it was about *motivation*. Turner needed Schorr. His priority wasn't to get Schorr on the best possible terms, but to provide Schorr with adequate incentives to join an organization Schorr had good reasons to distrust. Such scruples don't vanish overnight, and following Ted Turner down the press conference, and having just secured the deal of a lifetime, Daniel Schorr could still be heard muttering that he'd signed away a hard-won reputation. Nevertheless Turner had got his man.

Though complex, the nature of motivation can be stated very simply:

$$MOTIVATION \rightarrow EFFORT \rightarrow GOAL\text{-}ATTAINMENT$$

To say that someone is motivated is to say that he or she is willing to make the effort to reach a specific goal. Motivation and effort are like forces pressing against one another. The motive is something you want, while the effort is the amount of bother you will have to go to, or the amount of money you will have to pay, in order to get it. If the motive is strong (say, you need information from someone) and the effort is small (all you have to do is pick up the phone) you'll reach your goal almost without thinking. If the effort is greater (say, the person can be reached only by fax) and the motive is weak (you can get by without contacting him) then the goal will remain unfulfilled.

Motivation is so natural to us that most of the time we barely notice it. In fact in most cases people don't stop to analyze their motives, or to ask why a certain goal should attract them. Often it's near the truth to say that people 'don't really know what they want,' and that they could reach higher and more difficult goals if only they got their motives into shape. Solving the 'motive-muddle' lies at the heart of self-motivation, a key part of which is articulating to yourself what you really want, and then repeatedly bringing it to mind. When I put up a notice in my study targeting a certain level of return on my investments, I'm not just setting a goal; I'm saying to myself, 'That's what I want to attain.' Knowing I want it makes me more willing to expend the effort to get there.

Motivating others

In business relationships, though, the key skill isn't motivating yourself, but motivating *other people*. Good management, good leadership and good sales technique all depend on the same thing – being able to influence others in such a way that they choose to put more of their effort into achieving your chosen goal. In putting his case to Daniel Schorr, it's notable how Ted Turner made much of the fact that CNN would embody principles Schorr already believed in. This ability to show that other people's goals are met within your goal is basic to success in a variety of business practices:

▐ Getting selected for a job.
▐ Persuading a potential client to buy your product.
▐ Team building.
▐ Management of employees.
▐ Presentations to clients and superiors.

Having motivating power means finding another person's 'hot button.' Anyone setting out to motivate others wants to obtain enthusiastic, heart-and-soul support. But whether another person gives that is entirely up to them. Responses grade down from 'enthusiastic' through 'fairly keen' and 'half-hearted' to 'grudging' and 'only-under-duress.' You have no direct control over other people's decision-making. Indeed, any attempt at coercion will almost certainly backfire and produce resentment and intransigence. All you can do in motivating others is make as clear a link as possible between the goals you want them to share and the desires that most powerfully drive them. Get it wrong, and you'll spark no interest at all. Get it right, and they'll be motivating themselves.

The former Chairman of ICI put it in a nutshell when speaking of his own management style:

> I'm just a hired hack – a professional manager, I'm proud of that – I'm not a proprietor, not dominant. I lead by example and persuasion and a hell of a lot of hard work. Not on the basis of power or authority. My skills are to help a large number to release their energies and focus themselves. It is switching on a lot of people and helping them to achieve a common aim. People only do things they are convinced about. One has to create conditions in which people want to give of their best.[2]

The verbs stand out: *releasing* energies, *focusing, switching on.* The energy lies in the wires – all the effective leader can hope to do is locate the switch. Four points to bear in mind, though, in the art of motivation:

▪ **PEOPLE WANT DIFFERENT THINGS.** Motivation is complex because people want so many different things, and yet don't always rank them in the same order of importance. So while some motives are fairly universal – most people, for instance, being attracted by a good salary – others will vary depending on a person's character, age, gender and situation. Because you can't read other people's minds, you sometimes have to feel your way, as Ted Turner did with Daniel Schorr. But you can be sure that no two people will have their hot buttons in exactly the same place.

■ **YOU ARE PART OF THE MOTIVATION PACKAGE.** Like it or not, part of your motivating power rests on whether others see you as someone whom they find worthy of following. That's as true in a job interview as it is in the office of CEO, and it's why reputation, integrity and credibility have such a powerful effect on others' willingness to go with you.

■ **YOU CAN ACT IN A WAY THAT FACILITATES MOTIVATION.** By extension, how you treat those around you produces one of the strongest elements in personal motivating power. Whether you respect their face-needs. Whether you make them feel important. Whether you listen. Whether you take their complaints and anxieties seriously. Whether you behave graciously under fire. Conduct yourself well, and you will win people to your side.

■ **YOU CAN DEMOTIVATE AS WELL AS MOTIVATE.** By the same token it's possible to press 'cold' buttons as well as 'hot' ones. You can appeal to the wrong motives; set up goals that bear no relation to people's needs; lose their respect; act in a way that discourages them and makes them feel unwanted, undervalued and small. In motivation there is no neutral ground. You affect others whether you intend to or not. The question is: are you encouraging effort, or stifling it?

Ways to apply motivating power

Know what makes people tick

When you try to get another person interested in working toward a given set of goals, he or she will always ask 'What's in it for me?' If you can show the person that the goals will give them what they want, you will have succeeded in motivating them. So what do people want?

Since World War Two, thinking in this area has been dominated by Abraham Maslow, who theorized that all individuals seek to meet certain basic needs:

- **FULFILLMENT NEEDS** (growth, achievement, advancement)
- **EGO NEEDS** (recognition, status, self-respect)
- **SOCIAL NEEDS** (companionship, affection, friendship)
- **SECURITY NEEDS** (safety, security, stability)
- **PHYSICAL NEEDS** (food, shelter, health)

If we translate this wholesale into the world of work, we find that these categories cover the various kinds of question people ask themselves about their jobs:

FULFILLMENT
Is the job challenging?
Am I allowed to use my creativity?
Are there opportunities for advancement?
Can I achieve anything in this job?

EGO
Does the job have cachet?
Am I paid what I deserve?
Are my achievements recognized?
Do I have enough responsibility?

SOCIAL
Do superiors treat me well?
Do I have compatible colleagues?
Do I have friends at work?

SECURITY
Is the workplace safe?
Are there fringe benefits?
Are there general salary increases?
Is my job secure?

PHYSICAL

Is the workplace warm/cool enough?

Is my salary sufficient?

Are there adequate amenities?

Are my hours/conditions satisfactory?

Traditionally people are thought to prioritize these 'from the bottom up.' When in desperate straits, we think first of physical and security needs. Once these are looked after, social needs take precedence, and only once a stable social environment has been established are we likely to prioritize reputation and personal fulfillment. Also, which needs preoccupy a person will depend to some extent on personality. Some, for example, value status (an ego need) more highly than having a challenging job (a fulfillment need), while others put up with a cramped and stuffy workplace (which fails to meet a physical need) because they enjoy the camaraderie of working with others (a social need).

Identify needs in those who work for you

In an excellent study of leadership, the Director of the Xavier Institute of Management, Fr. Anthony d'Souza, has outlined some of the ways in which managers can pitch their interactions with employees to take into account these different categories of felt-need:[3]

Security need

HOW EMPLOYEES MAY BEHAVE:

- Tendency to be precise, orderly, systematic and tidy.
- Conscientious, intent on doing a good job.
- Tactful, diplomatic, cooperative and accommodating.
- Avoid antagonizing others.
- Interest in security programs and levels of benefits.

WHAT THEY ARE LOOKING FOR:

- Freedom from threats to their security.
- Avoidance of abrupt change.

▮ Sharing of responsibility.
▮ Clarity over job description and means to meet it.
▮ Predictable behavior by managers.
▮ Supportive leadership that shows how job should be done.
▮ Reassurance they're doing what's wanted and expected.

WHAT MANAGERS SHOULD DO:
▮ Provide clear instruction so employees know how to do their job.
▮ Encourage and build confidence.
▮ Give reassurance through praise.
▮ Provide support in times of difficulty.
▮ Explain coming changes carefully and well in advance.

Social need
HOW EMPLOYEES MAY BEHAVE:
▮ Friendly and outgoing.
▮ Close to family and group, on and off the job.
▮ Cooperative, willing, anxious to please.
▮ Good team members and workers.

WHAT THEY ARE LOOKING FOR:
▮ To be wanted and accepted, both professionally and personally.
▮ Evidence of their efforts being accepted and appreciated.
▮ Sincerity in relations with others.
▮ Notice of changes as a sign of good faith from managers.

WHAT MANAGERS SHOULD DO:
▮ Show sincere interest in people as individuals.
▮ Give periodic reassurance and praise for accomplishments.
▮ Exhibit concern by showing people ways to make the job easier.
▮ Involve people in effective group efforts.
▮ Solicit input before making changes.

Ego need
HOW EMPLOYEES MAY BEHAVE:
▮ Friendly and outgoing, often socially assertive.

- Good initiative-takers, often natural leaders.
- Poised, confident, at ease in new situations and with new people.
- Stimulated by variety of activities.
- Sometimes seek to be the center of attention.

WHAT THEY ARE LOOKING FOR:
- Recognition, status, popularity, attention.
- Variety in work and involvement in outside activities.
- Respect for their ability, knowledge, and accomplishments.
- Close identity with groups or organization.
- Resistant to regimentation and close control.

WHAT MANAGERS SHOULD DO:
- Provide opportunities for group work.
- Provide opportunities for variety and special projects.
- Provide opportunities for accomplishment.
- Recognize achievements.

Fulfillment need

HOW EMPLOYEES MAY BEHAVE:
- Keep up to date on their occupation.
- Look for problems to solve.
- Ask questions, then try to come up with improvements.
- Expect change to make sense – otherwise they question it.
- If change makes sense they adapt quickly.
- Emphasis on facts and objectivity.

WHAT THEY ARE LOOKING FOR:
- Challenge and stimulation.
- New assignments and problems to solve.
- Opportunities to do worthwhile work, to learn and to grow.

WHAT MANAGERS SHOULD DO:
- Provide exposure to new knowledge and work assignments.
- Set them to work on problem-solving projects.
- Consult them before making changes.

- Allow them to evaluate the need for change.
- Share relevant knowledge and coach for career development.
- Provide job opportunities in line with their self-development.

Recognize complex need

It's worth remembering, though, that most people don't fall neatly into one or another category. We all have complex and sometimes contradictory needs, for the following reasons:

- **NEEDS HAVE TRIGGERS**. Most people juggle all five categories of need at the same time, prioritizing a particular need only when it's in danger of going unmet. If your job becomes too repetitious you may suddenly register a fulfillment need for challenge and variety. If the air-conditioning fails in mid-July you'll quickly register a physical need for an ice-cold cola. Sometimes we barely know we have a need until circumstances reveal it to us.

- **NEEDS APPLY TO ALL OF LIFE**. Because people's energies go out in several directions – family, work, private pursuits – frustrations in one sphere can be compensated for in another. Those with unfulfilling jobs often find their fulfillment in hobbies, and others who are loners at work find their social needs met among family and non-work friends. Japanese corporations often set out to meet their employees' home and leisure needs as well as needs that are specifically work-related, even to the extent of providing company vacations. In Western corporations job-motivation is restricted far more to the workplace.

- **NEEDS VARY**. A need you downplay at one point in your career may become considerably more important at another. Typically, people about to have children will become more intensely aware of the need for job security.

- **NEEDS ARE TRADED ONE AGAINST ANOTHER**. 'Burning the midnight oil' to complete a report under the deadline is just one instance of sacrificing a lower need (in this case the physical need for rest) in order to satisfy a higher one (the ego need for recognition and reward). In other words, we sometimes ignore certain needs voluntarily if it suits us to do so.

This complexity doesn't stop us discerning what needs are uppermost in another person's mind – we just have to watch and listen a little harder. To take a simple example, it's sometimes assumed that customers in a retail store respond mainly to price (a physical need in the sense that they wish to conserve their money for other uses). But someone trying on a new pair of shoes may just as easily want shoes that last (a security need), shoes that are in fashion (a social need), or shoes that look expensive (an ego need). The retail assistant's ability to read the customer plays a vital part in the sale. The customer will sell *himself* the shoes, so long as the retail assistant can establish that the shoes on sale at the shop meet the customer's felt needs.

Get your goal across

The motivator Les Giblin tells the story of Charlie McCormick, who in the depths of the Great Depression took over what was then the world's largest spice and extract business. His uncle had been a hard boss, pushing sales up to $3.5 million in 1932 at the cost of a listless workforce that turned over at a rate of 30 per cent per year. It was just after he'd slashed wages by 25 per cent to off-set falling profits that the 'Old Man' suddenly died on a business trip, and the board elected Charlie to the chair. Immediately, records Giblin:

He called a meeting of all employees and announced a 10 per cent raise and a work week shortened from 56 to 46 hours. He also told the workers they had to raise production and cut costs or the whole kit and caboodle might collapse. To help them along he told his astonished employees they would henceforth share in the profits of the company and take an active part in management.[4]

Giblin makes the point that this change of style to what would now be called participative management had a dramatic effect. In twenty years Charlie McCormick increased his sales volume fifteen times to around $50m per year. Just as important, the 'junior board' of workers McCormick charged with the tasks of redesigning and modernizing the plant's working methods came up with more than 5,000 suggestions, of which a staggering 99 per cent were adopted by the senior board. 'I cannot estimate,' Giblin reports McCormick as saying, 'how much these suggestions have meant to this company in increased sales and profits, but certainly the benefits far exceed the cost.'

Modern management hasn't wised up to this lesson as much as it likes to think. McCormick's secret was to redefine the company's goals in such a way that the employees could own them. What he called 'the whole kit and caboodle' suddenly became common property and a joint responsibility. His employees were no longer functionaries hired to turn out so many bottles of spice per day; they were partners in the enterprise of making the company a success. That difference was crucial. McCormick had successfully transferred his goals, and because his employees suddenly identified those goals as their own, they willingly expended all the effort required to achieve them.

The situation in McCormick's company can be seen replicated across most of the globe. In a general way motivation is implicit in a work contract. Though workers may have no sense of ownership over the company's goals, they will still expend effort to reach them because they know this effort will be rewarded with a wage packet. The problem is, such implicit motivators aren't always motivating *enough*. In particular:

■ Regular wages are often taken for granted and thus lose their motivational power.
■ Even high wages tend not to motivate strongly if people have no personal commitment to corporate goals.

∎ The work may satisfy too few needs.
∎ Workers may not appreciate the connection between the
  work they do and the needs it might fulfill.

Part of the task of 'transferring goals' must address itself to overall company policy. That's why Charlie McCormick altered the
wage-structure of his company, and widened his workers'
responsibilities so they could meet not only their physical and
social needs but also their ego and fulfillment needs. Real policy
motivators of this kind have been widely adopted in the form of
bonus schemes, performance-related pay, commission on sales,
and worker-management schemes.

On a day-to-day basis, though, the transferring of goals
to others depends less on company policy than on personal
communication style. For example, 'Come in, Joe, I've got a job
for you to do' instills in Joe a mild sense of dread that he's about
to miss his coffee break while running some unwanted errand.
In the language of a previous chapter, it's a negative face-threat.
By contrast, 'Come in, Joe, I'd like your opinion on something'
fills Joe's heart with delight that his opinion is thought worth
soliciting. The second motivates; the first doesn't.

Effective motivation at this level has three elements:

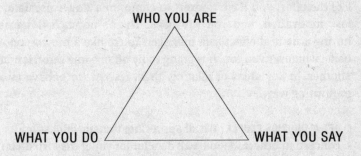

WHO YOU ARE

WHAT YOU DO   WHAT YOU SAY

These can be expressed differently as three principles:

- You will never motivate people if you fail to inspire their confidence as a person who is genuinely interested in their betterment.
- You will never motivate people if your actions don't match your words.
- You will never motivate people if your manner toward them is inappropriate to their perception of proper behavior.

Figure 2 outlines some of the main ways in which the style of verbal approach affects motivating power. Notice that they grade down from explicit commands, in which the goal is bluntly stated and the person expected to act, to requests in which the person is asked to help decide the means by which a goal should be attained, or even to help formulate the goal itself. These are not right and wrong management techniques – though few companies now run on military lines; rather they represent a range of communication styles the manager can draw from to suit a particular individual or situation.

As with all aspects of communication, verbal approach is a two-edged sword. Used rightly, it will motivate those around you; used wrongly, it will *demotivate* them. There's actually very little middle ground. The effort required to reach goals is a bit like the effort you have to exert to climb up a 'down' escalator: lose motivation, and you slip back. There's no such thing as having a neutral effect as a manager. You're like a moving pool ball – whatever you touch is going to fly off in some direction or another. In key areas of relating, then, it's vital to behave in a motivating way:

- **GET ALONGSIDE PEOPLE**. We all appreciate thoughtfulness and concern in others. People will do a lot for you if they trust you and know you have their best interests at heart. If you manage others, make the effort to find out about them and relax with them. Don't be chummy with your peers and shun those further down the management line – remember, everyone deserves equal respect.

FIGURE 2: Ways of expressing requests

'Do this.'
ORDER. Goal imposed.
Problem: Negative face-threat creates resentment.

'Please do this.'
POLITE ORDER. Goal imposed with politeness.
Problem: Politeness doesn't neutralize negative face-threat.

'I'd like you to do this.'
IMPLIED ORDER. Goal imposed, with implied option to refuse.
Problem: Weak request may not be acted on.

'Do this, or I will take action against you.'
THREAT. Goal imposed and widened to include punishment
   avoidance.
Problem: Focuses attention on possible sanctions.

'If you do this I will reward you.'
BRIBE. Goal imposed and widened to include extrinsic reward.
Problem: Focuses attention on reward.

'If you do this, the results will benefit you.'
PERSONAL INCENTIVE. Goal imposed with reminder of intrinsic
   reward to the individual.
Problem: Depends on individual's ability to visualize end-benefits.

'If you do this, the results will benefit everyone.'
GENERAL INCENTIVE. Goal imposed with reminder of intrinsic reward
   to the group.
Problem: Individual may be more concerned about self than group.

'How would you go about doing this?'
METHOD-FORMULATION. Goal imposed with method of achieving
   goal left open.
Problem: Demands creative response.

'Do you think this is worth doing?'
OBJECTIVE-APPRAISAL. Goal suggested but left open to amendment.
Problem: Value-assessment can weaken visionary power of the goal.

'What do you think we should do?'
OBJECTIVE-FORMULATION. Goal unformulated.
Problem: Can produce inadequate solutions.

■ **TELL PEOPLE WHAT YOU WANT.** It always helps to give precise instructions. Without clear objectives to work for, people lose respect for managers. They duplicate their work, slack off, squabble over procedures, and claim ignorance of instructions when held to account. So communicate clearly and well in advance. If possible, use a written directive. Let the person read it in your presence, and ask if he or she has questions you can answer.

■ **BE REASONABLE.** Be careful to ask of people what you know they can do, what will stretch them a little, but not what lies beyond their powers. Unattainable goals discourage people. They can't see the point of trying, and the quality of their work suffers. Make a careful assessment of those you manage, to ensure that you stretch them without breaking them.

■ **BE IMPARTIAL.** It's OK to be friends with everyone. It's not OK to be seen to give close friends preferential treatment. In particular, take care to remain impartial over complaints. Nothing destroys a manager's credibility more quickly than the suspicion that he or she favors particular people and bends the rules to protect them.

■ **KEEP HIGH EXPECTATIONS.** Expect nothing, and you'll get exactly nothing. So make it clear that you have confidence in others. Let them sense your faith in them; they will usually perform in line with your expressed confidence. Be ready to try out new ideas with them, and look out for opportunities to further their professional skills and give them greater responsibility.

■ **GIVE SPACE.** Organize, delegate, and then step aside. People need supervision and support, but they also need to feel you trust them enough to let them get on with the job. Once you've decided a person is capable of doing what you ask, set a time to review the project together, then let him or her get to it. But don't become invisible. Delegate but don't abdicate. If you appear distant, or fail to require accountability, you'll encourage sloppiness, broken deadlines, and time-wasting when people should be focused and on-task.

■ **WORK AT LISTENING**. Focus on what people say to you. And give verbal responses to help them along. Listen to what the person is saying, not to your preconceptions about the speaker. Avoid the temptation to butt in before they've made their point. Try to see the situation from their point of view, and empathize without losing your ability to see the situation objectively. Good listening is the first step to understanding another person's problems and putting those problems right. Failing to listen will increase frustration and cause loss of confidence.

■ **DON'T JUMP ON SMALL MISTAKES**. People worried about making mistakes seldom perform well. They work to the book, act evasive when questioned, and refuse to come clean when discussing problems. Try to set up a culture of non-blame. Make sure you pick up mistakes only when they're important, and handle fallout with discretion. Only in the most extreme circumstances hand out reprimands in public. This humiliates and creates resentment.

■ **DON'T TALK ABOUT OTHERS BEHIND THEIR BACKS**. Always give others the benefit of the doubt. Don't allow yourself the luxury of inflating your ego at the expense of somebody else's reputation. This bad practice creates division, and will almost always boomerang back at you. Rifts opened in seconds can take years to heal.

■ **DON'T CAUSE NEEDLESS OFFENSE**. Carelessness often undermines potentially good relationships. Despite the fact that women now occupy a place on most corporate boards, men still have an unfortunate habit of calling the chair the chair*man*, and of treating all female colleagues as promoted secretaries. Sensitivity in using appropriate language identifies you as a professional and wins support. Best to make the effort.

■ **PRAISE AT EVERY VIABLE OPPORTUNITY.** At a personal level, praise is one of the most powerful motivators a manager can use. It builds up self-esteem and heightens performance. But for that reason it should not be overused. Praising someone too much, or when they know they don't deserve it, will cause embarrassment and mistrust. If someone has produced mixed results, look for the points at which they have performed well and use your commendation of those points as a way of motivating broad-based improvement. Praise the performance not the person.

Summary and action plan

The principles of leadership that General William Slim later took into industry were hammered out on the field of battle. In 1943 Slim took command of the British Fourteenth Army, driven back into India by the Japanese and needing far-reaching repairs to its morale. Later, Slim wrote:

> Morale is a state of mind. It is that intangible force which will move a whole group of men to give their last ounce to achieve something, without counting the cost to themselves; that makes them feel they are part of something greater than themselves. If they are to feel that, their morale must, if it is to endure – and the essence of morale is that it should endure – have certain foundations. These foundations are spiritual, intellectual, and material. Spiritual first. Because only spiritual foundations can stand real strain. Next intellectual, because men are swayed by reason as well as feeling. Material last – important, but last – because the highest kinds of morale are often met when conditions are lowest.[5]

Slim went on to unpack these three ideas in the following way:

Spiritual
- There must be a great and noble object.
- Its achievement must be vital.
- The method of achievement must be active and aggressive.
- People must feel that what they are and what they do matters directly towards the attainment of the object.

Intellectual
- People must be convinced that the object can be obtained; that it is not out of reach.
- They must see, too, that the organization to which they belong, and which is striving to attain the object, is an efficient one.
- They must have confidence in their leaders, and know that whatever hardships they are called upon to suffer, their interests will not be forgotten or their support taken for granted.

Material
- People must feel that they will get a fair deal from their superiors.
- They must, as far as humanly possible, be given the best equipment for the task.
- Their working conditions must be made as good as they can be.

Group morale and personal motivation are closely related. They fire the effort needed to attain certain goals. In turn, whether certain goals are attained by an organization will depend on how effectively its leaders can associate those goals with the felt needs of those whose energy and efforts they wish to use. Business is not a slave ship. If you want to get the best out of people, do it by persuasion, not force.

The check-list for motivating power therefore includes the following:

1 Recognize the range of needs – physical, security, social, ego and fulfillment needs – that people wish to satisfy, and the

ways in which the desire to satisfy certain needs expresses itself in certain patterns of behavior.

2 Seek to give others the opportunity to satisfy more and higher needs through their work. The more satisfied a person is, the more productive he or she will be.

3 Any time you want to get another person 'on board' with a project, consider how you can best transfer your goals – defining your objectives in ways that directly or indirectly meet his or her felt need.

4 Concentrate on perfecting personal management skills – cultivating respect, giving support – that will encourage others to work hard and to take a pride in what they do.

5 Remember that motivating power must be exercised constantly. People who aren't motivated quickly become demotivated.

Notes

1 The following two quotes are taken from Douglas K. Ramsey, *The Corporate Warriors* (London: Grafton Books, 1987), pp.14–16.

2 Quoted in John Adair, *Great Leaders* (Guildford: Talbot-Adair Press, 1989), p.221.

3 See Fr. Anthony d'Souza, SJ, *Developing the Leader Within You: Strategies for Effective Leadership* (Singapore: Haggai Center for Advanced Leadership Studies, 1994), pp.282ff. I am grateful to Dr. d'Souza for many of the insights contained in this chapter.

4 Les Giblin, *How to Have Confidence and Power in Dealing with People* (Englewood Cliffs: Prentice Hall, 1964), p.122.

5 Adair, *Great Leaders*, p.105.

CHAPTER 6

Negotiation

What is negotiation?

On 1 March 1982, in a private dining room at Manhattan's exclusive Links club on East 62nd Street, a secret and highly unusual meeting took place between two arch-rivals in the global motor business – Eiji Toyoda, chairman of Japan's largest automobile company, Toyota, and the chairman of General Motors, Roger Smith. During dinner the conversation was casual, touching briefly on concerns that the American Congress would impose import restrictions on Japanese goods – a move most US motor manufacturers favored. Only after dinner did the two men get down to business.

Bringing out charts and briefing papers, Smith outlined a proposal that would revolutionize the American car industry. GM was the world's largest auto manufacturer; Toyota was the world's largest exporter. Why, said Smith, should the two companies not build passenger cars in the United States *together*?

In making his presentation, Smith highlighted three aims he knew to be central to the Japanese company's thinking about expansion into the US:

▪ To enter into a partnership before building cars in the United States.

▪ To sell more cars in the US market without having to cut back exports from Japan.

▪ To be sole manager of a joint operation.

Smith was forthright about the advantages for GM. It would allow his company to convert a former assembly plant into a modern facility operating under Japanese manufacturing systems, and in so doing give him access to the latest Japanese auto-manufacturing technology. It was, in a sense, an admission that American auto-production no longer led the global field. But Smith wasn't so candid about other benefits he saw coming out of the deal. According to one analyst, this venture was more than an attempt to buy into Japanese technology:

> It was to become the cornerstone of a new strategy in small cars aimed at pulling buyers not only out of 'import' showrooms, including Toyota's, but away from domestic small cars built by Ford and Chrysler as well. What Smith *didn't* tell Toyota at their meeting was that he considered the joint venture a stopgap solution to GM's problems. The temporary action would give Smith and General Motors more time to create a strategic plan to compete directly with the Japanese.[1]

The two sides of Western negotiation

In business, as in every part of life, negotiation begins from the fact that people need each other. Buyers need sellers, managers need workers, entrepreneurs need investors. Every working relationship is defined by some form of agreement, and every agreement results from a process of negotiation. It may be as simple a matter as two colleagues planning a meeting ('I'll address point 3 on the agenda, you address point 4'), or it may be a protracted series of discussions requiring whole teams of negotiators and designed to hammer out the terms of a corporate merger.

Until recently, Westerners have had two main approaches to negotiation. People negotiating informally with friends tend to be trusting and indulgent. They value the relationship, and do not wish to endanger it by being seen to 'drive a hard bargain.' Sometimes this concessionary approach will extend further – an example being the readiness of employees in a small firm to curtail wage demands in the interests of keeping the company solvent.

For the most part, though, once negotiation moves outside the context of a close-knit group, a second, and far tougher approach to negotiation takes over. The bargaining process becomes combative – a zero-sum game in which one party's gain is the other's loss. Anyone who's bought a second-hand auto-mobile will have had this experience of negotiation-as-combat. In fact, writers on negotiation often adopt the language of war-fare. The parties are 'opponents' who employ 'tactics' and 'maneuvers' in order to be 'winners' rather than 'losers.' And, as illustrated in the GM/Toyota example, there is a good deal of propagandizing, posturing, and concealment of intent.

But although this combative model of negotiation is still widely practiced, it has three major disadvantages:

■ **IT TENDS TO PRODUCE A NARROW FOCUS.** Combative negotiation begins with solutions. The seller declares a price of $X, the buyer offers $Y. Both 'positions' provide a solution to the buyer's and seller's joint problem of attaching a trade value to a given product or service. If, as is usually the case, these solutions differ, the next stage of negotiation consists of an argument in which each party attempts to persuade the other that it's own position is more reasonable. The creative thinking in the deal, therefore, revolves around bringing together two stated positions through compromise, and tends not to open out into a potentially more productive discussion of the needs the parties are attempting to satisfy. On the contrary, declaring what you 'really want' in combative negotiation is seen as giving away strategic information and thus putting yourself at a disadvantage. For example, knowing what Roger Smith 'really wanted' (leverage against Japanese car importers) would not have warmed Eiji Toyoda into accepting Smith's proposal.

■ **IT TENDS TO BREED DIRTY TRICKS.** Since people go into combative negotiation with the aim of securing the best deal they can for their own party, there is pressure to use 'unfair' procedural and psychological techniques to get the other side to comply. Experiments have shown, for instance, that sellers who pitch their opening bid artificially high are likely to achieve a more satisfactory final sale-price than those whose opening bid is lower. Out on the dealership lot, the unscrupulous car salesman knows that, by asking $8,000 for a car he'd probably let go for $5,500, he will alter the customer's perception of the car's value and thus of what constitutes a 'good deal'.

■ **IT TENDS TO MAKE SUCCESS SUBJECTIVE.** Agreements ought to be settled on the basis of (a) a reasonably objective assessment of a product's value, and (b) a thorough knowledge of the needs an agreement is meant to satisfy. Where neither of these conditions hold, negotiators soon lose perspective and fail to distinguish between satisfactory and unsatisfactory outcomes. The negotiation expert Chester L. Karrass tells about a meeting he once had with an aerospace supplier. The supplier had put down a fixed-price bid of $450,000. Karrass's team would have been happy to settle at $425,000 – but opened at $140,000. They managed to win successive concessions, finally settling at midnight for $220,000. Because the supplier's negotiators felt they'd secured *the best deal possible in the circumstances*, Karrass recalls that they went away happy. But 'they will never know,' he adds, 'that they threw away over $200,000 at the table.'[2]

■ **IT TENDS TO PRODUCE ALIENATION.** This book has already noted the problems Western business people have had in forming effective working relationships in the developing world. Combative negotiating techniques have substantially contributed to this – and not just with less economically powerful partners. In Japanese business, for instance, negotiation has traditionally taken a more cooperative form. Buyers have the higher status in Japanese society. Consequently the seller gives the buyer most of what he asks for, in response to which, and in accordance with the principle of *amae*, the buyer accepts an obligation to 'look after' the seller. Unaware of this cultural nuance – and hungry for every concession they can get – American buyers in Japan have sometimes given Japanese sellers a beating.

Principled negotiation

A different approach to negotiation, simultaneously more productive and more resilient to combative opposition, has been developed by Fisher and Ury in their ground-breaking book *Getting to Yes*.[3] Their system of 'principled' or 'win-win' negotiation sets out a number of working procedures by which negotiators can avoid the pitfalls of zero-sum bargaining. In a business context these could be rendered as follows:

■ **EXPLAIN NEEDS, DON'T DEFEND POSITIONS.** Principled negotiation advocates disclosure. If you know what the other side values, you will be better placed to come up with a package they can accept. Also, it's often the case that the parties are already locked into a relationship – for instance, in internal wage bargaining – and that the quality of that relationship will have a tangible effect on future motivation and productivity.

■ **INVENT OPTIONS THAT BENEFIT BOTH SIDES.** Principled negotiation opens the way to joined-up solutions. On stopovers during grueling round-the-world tours I would often negotiate with a hotel to make temporary use of a room. I got a bed to sleep on for a couple of hours without paying the full day rate. The hotel covered its costs and made a little more than they'd have done by letting the room stay empty – plus they got a happy customer. Finding options requires flexibility of thought, and a realization that advantage takes a variety of forms. The price agreed for a product or service will change depending on what else is thrown into the deal. Speed of delivery. Quality. Size of order. Tie-ins. Commitments to future trade. Rarity. Publicity. Productivity. Credibility. Ease of application. An almost endless list of factors can have value and therefore have a bearing on what people see as a satisfactory 'package.' Occasionally the factor that clinches a deal may have nothing to do with organizational needs, and everything to do with the needs of the negotiator. After ten hours at the table, people have been known to sign away the stockroom out of sheer exhaustion.

■ **INSIST ON OBJECTIVE CRITERIA.** What matters in assessing the terms of an agreement is the real value of the benefits offered when set against the needs you wish to satisfy. You may be offered office space at a reduction of 15 per cent of the original asking price, but whether or not this constitutes a 'good deal' depends on hard criteria like closeness to transport links, overheads, state of repair, and suitability to purpose. It is against these, and not against the uncertain value of a supposed 'saving,' that the benefits of a proposal should be measured.

■ **NEVER GIVE IN TO PRESSURE.** You have no control over the tactics the other party might use in attempting to secure an agreement. You do, however, have real interests to defend and, in most situations, an effective power of veto. So-called dirty tricks are cheap and unprofessional. If negotiation is a game – as many like to think – the first requirement must be that people play by the rules. If they don't, the principled negotiator has every right to call them to account.

Ways to apply negotiation

Protect relationships from power

When the British publishing magnate Robert Maxwell had his showdown with the Mirror Group printing unions in 1985, he opened his attack by letting it be known (1) that the paper *Sporting Life* would be sold, and (2) that he might close the old printing plant and institute a completely new arrangement of out-sourced and strike-free printing. The unions agreed to talks, and after two days of what one union negotiator described as 'constant aggression, constant attack,' Maxwell emerged with a partial agreement. But he wasn't satisfied. Eight weeks later, according to Maxwell's biographer Tom Bower:

> Maxwell claimed that the September agreement for uninterrupted production had been broken and announced that unless the unions agreed to an immediate cut of 2,000 out of the 6,500 jobs, of whom 1,100 were over sixty years old, the *Mirror* would close. Every employee was issued with a dismissal notice.[4]

The new Employment Act, with its restrictions on strike action, and Maxwell's ability to make good his threat to close the paper, shifted the balance of power decisively in Maxwell's favor. The union leaders began to cower. Maxwell imposed another deadline of 10 December, and then

> corralled all the negotiators into a number of rooms to discuss how they would meet his demands. By the final day, he had achieved an overwhelming victory. Most of the overmanning and excesses would disappear; 2,100 employees were made redundant and their payments would be largely funded from the surplus in their pension fund.

Power balances underlie all negotiation, and in some circumstances, like the above, power lies so firmly on one side of the table that the powerful party can push through its program virtually unresisted. On what occasions this is a right or useful or appropriate thing to do is not a question I'm concerned with here. But three things should be noted:

1. A balance of power can have several sources

Power itself is a complex matter. A working definition of it would be 'the ability to make others decide of their own free will to comply with your wishes.' You have a power *dis*advantage if any of the following circumstances apply:

▪ The other party's veto or non-cooperation would leave you with less gain than you might otherwise expect. Power derives from the ability to spoil, and can be present, paradoxically, even when in other respects a party appears almost completely powerless. A typical instance is the debtor who can force creditors to settle for minimal repayments in preference to receiving nothing at all.

▪ You are more heavily committed to the business relationship than the other party is. This simply means you have more to lose, and will by the same token be more motivated to accept terms that keep the relationship intact.

▪ You lack options. This was what finally gave Robert Maxwell leverage over the union leaders. It's one of the basics of bargaining that buyers with multiple sources can bid up the price. A buyer can further reduce the seller's power by arranging to manufacture the product rather than buy it in, and a seller can similarly reduce a buyer's options by developing uniquely desirable qualities in the product which cannot be obtained elsewhere.

▪ Others know more about you than you know about them. Another basic of bargaining: the more another party knows about your objectives and financial constraints, the firmer the grip he or she will have on your decision-making. If the other party knows your bottom-line price is $1.5m, you'll be lucky to negotiate $1.6. Additional aspects of information-power include understanding of contextual issues like legal and fiscal systems and 'going rates' for the commodity you're attempting to buy or sell.

▌ You're unwilling to make the effort. Stamina is an essential ingredient of business success, as Robert Maxwell knew. It's easy to forgo thorough planning, just as it's easy to let deadlock nudge you into making a quick agreement. Not surprisingly, an effort well worth making in business is the acquisition of bargaining skill.

2. There is a difference between apparent and real power

Because power is viewed as crucial in combative negotiation, people whose advantage is marginal in real terms will often attempt to swing the other party behind their proposals by exaggerating the degree of their advantage. Former ITT boss Harold Geneen tells a story of his negotiation with Honeywell, necessitated by his company's need to extricate itself from a previous agreement which imposed severe penalties for withdrawal. Geneen recalls:

> I met with the chief executive of Honeywell, and insisted that the only way Honeywell could get free and clear control over the venture was to buy us out for our full investment. Otherwise, I told him, we would be obliged to sell our shares in the computer company to the public. Then if the product failed as a Honeywell-controlled subsidiary, the embarrassment to Honeywell would be widespread. It was almost complete bluff. But Honeywell was persuaded to buy us out for our full investment.[5]

Needless to say, this sort of ruse is most likely to work on you if you've already disadvantaged yourself by failing to research your position thoroughly.

3. Power play in negotiation carries a high price

Blatant exploitation of power almost always degrades the relationship between the parties, damaging the foundation of trust on which future cooperation depends. In the rounds of furious cost-cutting at Robert Maxwell's corporation BPC, for instance, Maxwell's imperious management style cost him many of his best executives. According to Tom Bower, 'They were weary and wary of an instant decision-maker, "shooting from the hip", who rejected the conventional organization of management and who seemed to thrive on creating rather than settling uncertainty.' One top manager 'calls it "motivation by fear" and, among other reasons, left because "I couldn't stand wondering when the stab would come."' [6]

Most people see power as an asset in negotiation. But in many ways it has less long-term significance than the goodwill of the other party. Power balances can shift abruptly according to circumstance; but once lost, goodwill is not easily regained. And the heavy-handed use of power-advantage is often to blame where goodwill has been thrown away. For that reason, good negotiators make sparing use of power as a motivator, and go to considerable trouble to set up conditions which maximize comfort, parity and clear communications.

Cecil Day, founder of Days Inn Motels, once wanted to buy a piece of property owned by a farmer. He asked the farmer his price. When the farmer responded, Cecil replied, 'I don't think you realize how land values have escalated.' He insisted on giving the farmer far more than the farmer asked. Cecil believed that a good deal must be fair and profitable for both parties. That may be one reason why, of the hundreds of Motel franchises he sold, not one litigated a claim against him.

Set up a level playing field

Long before you reach the point of face-to-face negotiation, ensure that your encounter with the other party won't be structured in such a way as to confer obvious and unfair advantage. In particular:

▪ **PICK THE RIGHT VENUE.** Inconvenient or uncomfortable conditions don't underscore your professionalism. If you are providing the venue, make sure the seating is adequate for a full day's use. Check that there are toilets and private rooms on hand, and ensure a ready supply of refreshments and rest-breaks. Also, take care how you arrange the furniture. Sitting the parties on opposite sides of a conference table implies conflict; sitting in a circle or horseshoe, or, in the Japanese style, facing a wall where all relevant information can be displayed, helps to establish a mood of collaboration.

▪ **PICK THE RIGHT TEAM.** Never place people on your negotiating team simply to intimidate. Every member should have a function – covering all relevant areas of expertise and, not least important, an observer who is able to give a more independent view and read the other team while members of your own are doing the talking. Try to match the other team in terms of seniority, not least because this can help to ensure equal levels of decision-making power. Remember that in Eastern cultures, particularly, the status of team members will also be taken as a sign of the seriousness of your intent, and that sending young people to negotiate with their elders is likely to cause insult. Be aware that some cultures accord high degrees of respect to certain professions (teachers, for instance, have high status in Korea).

▪ **PICK THE RIGHT TIME.** Western negotiators often make the mistake of setting deadlines for the reaching of agreement. Deadlines can have the effect of concentrating minds. But they can also make you hostage to your timetable. In the East, particularly, it is unwise to indicate any degree of urgency. Negotiation produces uncertainty, and most people have a natural urge to resolve uncertainty as soon as possible. Indeed, Americans have occasionally played into the hands of an Eastern negotiating party by imposing a tight timeframe, and thus placing undue pressure on themselves to settle.

Play hard, play fair

Just as important as setting up the right conditions for negotiation is managing the negotiating relationship while discussions are going on. A study comparing the behavior of 'skilled' and 'average' negotiators in Britain suggests some practical do's and don'ts when it comes to relating across the table:[7]

- **AVOID ANNOYING CLICHES.** Using terms like 'generous offer' and 'fair price' have no real 'cash value'. If they have any effect at all it is only to annoy people. Average negotiators use 10.8 per hour, skilled negotiators a sparing 2.8.

- **DON'T ANSWER PROPOSALS WITH PROPOSALS.** This indicates that you are either not intelligent enough to understand the other party's proposal, or not polite enough to tell them how it fails to meet your requirements. Average negotiators counter-propose 3.1 times per hour, skilled negotiators only 1.7.

- **DON'T LET YOURSELF BE BAITED.** Downward spirals of emotive accusation and defensive counterattack do nothing to bring agreement nearer. Average negotiators get drawn into them 6.3 per cent of the time, skilled negotiators only 1.9 per cent.

- **PUT OUT TRAILERS.** Phrases like 'Can I ask for clarification here ...?' placed before a question, comment or suggestion, help to focus what you say. Skilled negotiators use this 'behavioral labeling' 6.4 per cent of the time (average negotiators manage only 1.2%). The only exception occurs where negotiators are about to disagree. Here it is the average negotiators who give warning of their views (using redundant phrases like 'I'm not sure I go along with that'), while skilled negotiators come abruptly to the point (labeling disagreement in advance only 0.4% of the time).

- **USE ACTIVE LISTENING.** Repeat back what the other party has said in your own words, to verify that you've understood it. Skilled negotiators do this 7.5 per cent of the time, unskilled negotiators only 4.2 per cent.

■ **ASK QUESTIONS**. You don't learn if you don't ask. So don't fill in the blanks from your imagination, however well you think you 'read' situations. Ask for clarification. Skilled negotiators devote an amazing 21.3 per cent of their negotiating time to this, unskilled negotiators only 9.6 per cent.

■ **REFLECT BACK YOUR FEELINGS**. This is a way of communicating caution without putting the other party's back up. 'I feel very positive about that idea, but I also feel a slight unease about the figures it's based on. Can you help me resolve that ...?' Skilled negotiators do this 12.1 per cent of the time, average negotiators only 7.8 per cent.

■ **NEVER USE A WEAK ARGUMENT TO BOLSTER A STRONG ONE**. There may be two good reasons for doing something; there are rarely three. In fact, the more arguments you use to back up your case the stronger the suspicion will be that you've trimmed them to fit. Skilled negotiators use an average of 1.8 arguments to back each case. Average negotiators use three.

Have zero-tolerance for foul play

One of Harold Geneen's early posts was with Bell and Howell. In these post-war years the Office of Price Administration sought to cap soaring prices on scarce goods. The formula they used to do this excluded factors like engineering and R&D, which figured highly in Bell and Howell's costs. According to Geneen, word filtered down from the chief executive Joseph McNab to the effect that Geneen was to fill out the OPA forms in such a way that Bell and Howell got the price increases it needed on key camera models. Geneen had been with the firm barely a year. He knew this was a defining moment:

> There was no way I could do that without fudging the figures. And so I said. Word came back that Mr. McNab did not care how or what I did. He needed and wanted those price increases.

So I presented myself to him in his office, unannounced, and told him, 'I will not fill in your figures or anybody's figures incorrectly. But I'll tell you what I will do. I'll go to Washington and I'll plead our case under the hardship provisions of the OPA.'[8]

This was not well received, and Geneen swiftly retreated before McNab could say yes or no. He went to Washington. It took a week of tough talking, but he gave it his best, and phoned McNab to announce that he'd won an increase, not just on selected models, but 8 per cent on all Bell and Howell's prices across the board. McNab's response was a grunt. However, when McNab suddenly died five years later, he left instructions saying that Geneen should be kept on at all costs as financial head of the company.

Robert Maxwell had a reputation as a ruthless negotiator, his main technique being to make an agreement, and then to wear everyone down by renegotiating and haggling. Furthermore, when he became a newspaper proprietor he cowed most of his editorial staff by dictating the editorial positions the paper would take. Strangely, though, the employees who fared best were often the ones who refused to toe the line. As his biographer later commented, 'Maxwell ... respects those who resist his cajolery.'

The first law of negotiation is that doormats get walked on – and there are plenty of people out there who will try to squeeze a few extra concessions out of you by turning the screws. Basically, negotiating effectively against 'dirty tricks' requires a willingness to do three things:

■ Stand your ground.
■ 'Call' the other party on unfair tactics.
■ Define how fairness applies in particular instances.

Principled negotiators should always keep default solutions in mind. That is, if the other party refuses to play fair, you should be sufficiently on the ball to know whether a bad deal is better than no deal at all. Bear the cultural dimension in mind in all of this. All cultures have a moral foundation – a basis for understanding that some tactics are right and others wrong. At the same time, the dividing line between the two can shift as you move from one culture to another. High levels of body contact, for example, appear as intimidation to many Westerners used to maintaining their 'personal space'; whereas in Arabic cultures it is merely routine.

Some of the commoner forms of unfair tactic used in negotiation are these:

- **'I STILL NEED TO RUN THAT BY THE BOSS.'** Just as you think every loose end's been tied up, it turns out that someone 'upstairs' can come in and demand new concessions. There are two ways to counter this. (1) Remember to clarify at an earlier stage what decision-making powers the other party has. In some Eastern cultures, referral back to absent bosses is the norm. (2) Make it clear that you regard the agreement as provisional on *both* sides until 'the boss' is ready to ratify it. In other words, you politely reserve the right to make your own new demands if the other party wants to go that route.

- **'TAKE IT OR LEAVE IT.'** The other party makes a 'final offer,' involving concessions from you, and refuses to budge any further. In fact most final offers are nothing of the kind. If it really holds things up, remind the other party what they'll lose by abandoning the negotiation. Be aware of the face-issues at stake: you want them to come back into the negotiation, so it may be better simply to gloss over the 'final offer' and throw some new factor into the equation that opens the way for them to climb down.

- **'THAT'S ALL WE HAVE IN THE BUDGET.'** The budget is used as an alibi to save the other party making further concessions. In reality, though, budget priorities are just another factor in the negotiation – if the deal's good enough, money can usually be found to fund it. Don't make the mistake of setting yourself up for this one by under-quoting your estimated price at an earlier stage. And remember you can respond in kind by making it clear that the budgeted amount simply isn't economic for you.

■ **'WE HAVE OTHER SUPPLIERS TO GO TO.'** Dependency on a particular customer or supplier shifts the balance of power away from you and makes you more likely to agree to concessions. Coming from this position, the other party has a strong motive to cover up and pretend he or she has more options than is really the case. A thorough knowledge of the market helps a lot here. If the other party really *does* have alternative suppliers on the roster, do they all offer the same quality and service that you do?

■ **'PERSONALLY I'D AGREE TO THAT PRICE BUT MY PARTNER WON'T PLAY BALL.'** This is a variation on running the deal by the boss – except the payoff comes upfront because it's made clear that the partner/boss will drive a harder bargain. This is a cheap trick. If the partner's that tightfisted, he has no business sending someone else to negotiate on his behalf. Either the price is fair, or it's not. If the person you're talking to isn't empowered to negotiate a price, you should be dealing with the partner direct.

■ **'THE PRICE IS $250,000.'** When you know darn well the product is worth only $75,000. Extreme opening bids are customary in some cultures, where everyone understands the formality of overstating the case. The reasonable price, however, is determined not by what the other party initially demands, but by your objective estimate of what the product or service is worth. If the other party persists in overpricing, demand a breakdown to explain how they arrive at their figure.

■ **'THE PRICE IS $75,000.'** When it turns out after you've signed the deal that various unseen extras push the real price up to nearer $250,000. This tactic, sometimes called 'low-balling,' is pursued with the aim of eliminating competition and placing the customer in a position where it is cheaper to keep pace even with escalating costs than it is to pull out. If you suspect the other party has this in mind, insist on compliance clauses.

■ **'I'M STILL NOT SATISFIED WITH …'** When that part of the deal was cheerfully agreed on at an earlier stage. This tactic of using recent agreements to unbalance previous ones opens negotiation up to a never-ending cycle of revisions to which the weaker party may finally capitulate out of sheer fatigue. Robert Maxwell used the tactic to good effect. The remedy in Western business negotiation is firm refusal to go back over old ground. In many Eastern cultures, however, remember that agendas are pursued not point by point, like a train passing successive stations, but synoptically, taking all the issues at once. Revisiting one front in light of developments on another is therefore the norm.

Summary and action plan

Break business down, and what you're left with is a series of negotiated agreements. Some are formal, some are informal. In both cases the ability to negotiate effectively is a fundamental skill of business relating. Experience suggests that the best long-term deals are accomplished neither by *concessionary* bargaining, in which disproportionate emphasis is placed on preserving harmony in the relationship, nor by *combative* bargaining, in which equally disproportionate emphasis is placed on the winning of short-term advantage. Clearly good business relationships need harmony and mutual trust. But just as clearly good business relationships must be good in the sense that they meet the needs of both parties in the short term as well as the long.

A checklist for negotiating solutions in business will therefore cover the following:

1 Ensure that you take a principled approach to negotiation – taking into account needs on both sides, inventing options for mutual gain, insisting on objective criteria, and refusing to give in to pressure.

2 Be aware of power differentials – of who holds which cards – but place less importance on power play than on developing cooperation and goodwill as a basis for negotiation.

3 As far as you can, establish a 'level playing field,' setting up conditions for negotiation – in physical surroundings, choice of team members, use of time-frames – that increase the likelihood of cooperative behavior and mutually satisfactory outcomes.

4 Take care to manage relationships sensitively during negotiation, stressing such activities as active listening, clarification, questioning and politeness.

5 Do not engage in so-called dirty tricks, and do not tolerate their use by the other party. If unfair tactics are deployed against you, draw attention to them and negotiate to establish fair 'rules of the game.'

Notes

[1] Douglas K. Ramsey, *The Corporate Warriors* (London: Grafton Books, 1987), p.177. Other details of this GM–Toyota negotiation are taken from Ramsey's account.

[2] Chester L. Karrass, *The Negotiating Game* (New York: Thomas Y. Crowell, 1970), p.7.

[3] R. Fisher and W. Ury, *Getting to Yes* (Boston: Houghton Mifflin, and New York: Penguin, 1981).

[4] Tom Bower, *Maxwell: The Outsider* (London: Aurum Press, 1988), p.310.

[5] Harold Geneen with Alvin Moscow, *Managing* (New York: Doubleday, 1984), p.78.

[6] Bower, *Maxwell*, p.267.

[7] See Neil Rackham, *The Behavior of Successful Negotiators* (Reston, VA: Huthwaite Research Group, 1976).

[8] Geneen with Moscow, *Managing*, p.72.

CHAPTER 7

Conflict Utilization

What is conflict utilization?

Most people don't associate the word 'conflict' with Japanese industry. From the Western point of view, a Japanese corporation can give the impression of being monolithic, uniform and composed of employees whose highest concern centers on avoiding conflict and disfavor. If that is true, however, the former chairman of the Sony Corporation, Akio Morita, represents a departure from the norm. As he says:

> Many Japanese companies like to use the words *cooperation* and *consensus* because they dislike individualistic employees. When I am asked, and sometimes when I am not, I say that a manager who talks too much about cooperation is one who is saying he doesn't have the ability to utilize excellent individuals and their ideas and put their ideas in harmony.[1]

Morita wasn't afraid to put this philosophy into practice even with his own superiors. As deputy chairman of Sony his approach differed markedly from that of the chairman Michiji Tajima, an old-school company boss who also served as director general of the Imperial Household Agency, which handles the affairs of the Japanese royal family. Eventually, and inevitably, things came to a head:

Finally [Tajima] could stand it no longer and said, 'Morita, you and I have different ideas. I don't want to stay in a company like yours where you don't have the same ideas that I have and we are sometimes in conflict.'

I was very bold in my response because I felt as strongly then as I do now about this issue. I said, 'Sir, if you and I had exactly the same ideas on all subjects, it would not be necessary for both of us to be in this company and receive a salary. Either you or I should resign in that case. It is precisely because you and I have different ideas that this company will run a smaller risk of making mistakes.'[2]

Making use of conflict

Sooner or later, to a greater or smaller degree, all relationships run into problems. Some can start off on the wrong foot, as anyone will know who has walked into a new job. The seventh secret of effective business relating, then, must be the skill of preventing relationship breakdown becoming self-reinforcing and terminal.

Out of habit, we normally blame breakdown of relationships on conflict. Where conflict becomes the defining quality of a relationship, the 'social machinery' of the workplace will begin to bump and grind, and productivity will suffer. Decision-making takes too long. Discussions lead to pointless arguments and unresolved tension. People get demotivated and fail to reach organizational goals. Suspicion and distrust emerge as keynotes of working relationships. People stop talking. Teamwork becomes an effort. And soon, unhappiness in the workplace finds expression in resignations, requests for transfer, sick leaves, and a seemingly unending stream of 'fires' that higher management must waste time putting out.

All this might imply that conflict works entirely against the interests of business effectiveness. But three points should be remembered:

■ Conflict isn't the only way relationships can become dysfunctional in business. Just as much damage can be caused by people avoiding disagreements and obediently carrying out defective instructions. The effect is less dramatic, but it's just as powerful.

■ Conflict can't be avoided. It is part of the human condition that people get along in some ways and not in others. Conflict-free business simply doesn't exist. And, as Akio Morita rightly observed, diversity of viewpoints and approaches gives a company valuable competitive edge.

■ Conflict can be constructive. In that way it resembles combustion. Put a match to gasoline in the open air and you'll get an uncontrolled explosion. Ignite it inside an internal combustion engine and you'll have a car moving forward. The difference lies in the way we control the process.

So treat conflict in business relationships as a potential resource. Badly handled, it will burn out of control and do damage. Well handled, it can be made to serve a useful purpose. And handling conflict well means handling it not only in your own relationships, but also in the relationships of those working around you. A large part of the expertise you need in this area lies in awareness and careful planning. Knowing how to use a fire extinguisher may be useful, but a far more effective way to stop fires is to take care how you store your gasoline.

To summarize:

■ **KNOW WHERE CONFLICT COMES FROM.** Most conflict in work situations stays hidden. Either it remains too weak to motivate action, or individuals who might wish to act on it instead stay silent because they don't want to be branded as troublemakers. Not infrequently, then, apparently cordial office environments can hide strong undercurrents of resentment and dislike. Women, in particular, will often soak up a good deal of patronizing and sexist behavior by male colleagues simply in order to keep the peace. Other conflicts result from the pairing of employees who have very different psychological traits – a problem that can be foreseen and averted with the help of psychometric techniques like the Myers-Briggs test. Also, it's worth remembering that some kinds of conflict arise directly from management decisions – for example where two project managers have to compete for resources. Unless handled with great sensitivity, situations which create 'winners' and 'losers' will always result in a corrosion of relationships.

■ **KNOW WHAT THE TRIGGERS ARE**. Conflicts may surface slowly – or they may explode with little apparent warning. Either way we should make an effort to distinguish the real underlying causes of conflict from the triggers that release them. Michiji Tajima, for instance, didn't confront Akio Morita about their differing approaches to running Sony until Morita forced the issue by persistently stepping out of line. Similarly, personality clashes may stay hidden until two individuals have to collaborate. And generalized feelings of resentment against a manager may break out in a formal complaint only when that manager makes a new and unpopular decision. In all these cases, successfully handling the conflict requires addressing the problem at both levels. Putting on the safety lock may help in the short term, but it doesn't take the ammunition out of the gun. Too often, the same underlying condition of conflict will ignite again and again in a series of individual crises.

■ **KNOW HOW TO CHANNEL CONFLICT IN THE RIGHT DIRECTIONS**. A young manager in Sony once confided in Akio Morita, 'Before I joined this company ... I thought it was a fantastic company. It is the only place I wanted to work. But I work for this section chief, Mr. So-and-So, and in my lowly capacity I work for this man, not Sony. He represents the company. But he is stupid, and everything I do or suggest must go through this guy.' As a result, Morita began a weekly company newspaper to advertise internal job openings, and instigated a new policy of moving employees into related or new work about every two years. It had the useful payoff of keeping employees happy and of identifying problem managers. Morita rightly perceived the benefit behind the conflict. The young men chafing at the strictures imposed by an older superior represented an important asset for the company to develop. He didn't try to suppress the conflict. He used it for Sony's greater good.

Ways to apply conflict utilization

Engage, assert, respond

Potentially destructive conflict in the workplace usually falls into one of the following categories:

■ **STYLE: 'I DON'T LIKE THE WAY HE OR SHE WORKS.'** People have very different ways of tackling work projects. You may be meticulous and methodical; your colleague may work in apparent chaos. You may desire regular feedback; your boss may prefer to leave you to get on with your responsibilities. You may have a strong intuitive streak and take account of other people's feelings; someone you're working with may think almost entirely in terms of procedures and performance targets. Style differences often lead to conflict in situations where planning has been insufficiently exact. When things go wrong, failure focalizes the conflict, with one party claiming to have been let down by the other's inattention or negligence.

■ **VALUES: 'I DON'T LIKE HIS OR HER WHOLE APPROACH.'** Whereas with differences of style people can 'live and let live,' value differences go all the way down. If you have a strong career motivation, you may find yourself at odds with those whose family concerns and life outside the workplace lead them to list priorities differently. Value distinctions may cause one person to call another 'not really a team member,' and can also underlie disagreements about the way a company should be run, including overtime policy and complaints procedures. Similarly, value distinctions make possible the 'theft' of intellectual property. That most irritating occurrence of somebody passing off your good ideas as their own betrays a value difference between a person who respects right of ownership and a person who's on the take.

■ **PREJUDICE: 'I DON'T LIKE THE SORT OF PERSON HE OR SHE IS.'** You know things are going wrong when you hear people addressed as a category – 'people like you' or 'his or her kind.' And of course prejudice finds expression through body language, manner, exclusion and preferment even if the words are not used. In this way prejudice based on race continues to exert an influence in the workplace, as does prejudice based on disability, age or gender.

■ **SELF-ESTEEM: 'I DON'T LIKE THE WAY HE OR SHE TREATS ME.'** This differs from style, although it may be a symptom of prejudice. Damage to self-esteem results from poor use of facework, and occurs in situations where employees get bawled out, where office life is characterized by pettiness and thoughtlessness, and where people hand out criticism beyond the call of duty and without taking due account of its effects. Very often, behavior patterns like these reflect personal insecurity and a weak management style that perpetuates a culture of blame.

■ **DEPENDENCY: 'I DON'T LIKE HIM OR HER LEANING ON ME.'** Teamwork implies interdependence. That means people support one another, and help one another out in time of need. But governing the way we deploy this support are unseen principles of reciprocity and fairness. Constantly deferring to superiors for advice produces a negative face-threat and turns you into a 'burden.' Similarly, relying too much on your colleagues' goodwill for favors like delivering messages and tidying up your sales report will get you the reputation of a sponger.

▮ **TRIBALISM: 'I DON'T LIKE HIS OR HER ALLEGIANCE.'** Most of us have been in an office that's divided down the middle by petty politics. People who think things should change vs. people who like the status quo. People who feel an injustice has been done vs. people who don't want to rock the boat. People on the inside vs. people who feel marginalized. In the hothouse atmosphere of the typical office, your position on the chosen issue will determine who sees you as a friend and who sees you as a traitor. Standing above it all can be difficult.

Nearly all these forms of conflict get more convoluted if the relationship straddles two cultures. Studies of American firms operating in China during the 1980s show just how easily things can go wrong. At Babcock and Wilcox Beijing Company Ltd, Chinese employees evaluated their managers on the basis of their willingness to work the Americans. Those who quarreled aggressively were seen as comrades in arms, whereas those who cooperated would be nicknamed *Er Gui Zi*, or 'fake foreigners.'[3] Similar problems dogged Beijing Jeep, where even superficial disagreements quickly broke down into mutual recrimination.[4]

Very often relationship breakdown has more than one cause and takes more than one form. Sorting out the various strands can be time-consuming and difficult. Tackling a conflict situation effectively, however, begins from the fairly simple foundation shown in Figure 3. It comes down to clear communications:

▮ **ASSERTIVENESS** – You need to respect your own needs, establishing your own position clearly so that the other person can understand it.

▮ **RESPONSIVENESS** you need to respect the needs of the other person, listening actively to the other person's point of view.

Your ability to keep these elements both in play and in balance determines how effective you'll be in resolving the conflict.

FIGURE 3: Assertiveness and responsiveness in conflict utilization

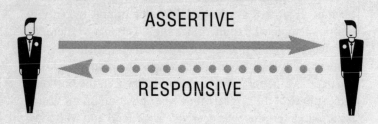

Broadly, as Figure 4 indicates, you will find yourself taking one of four approaches.

Dominance

There are good reasons for being assertive, both in terms of your own wellbeing and the success of your business. For example, research demonstrates that assertiveness:

- Gives you a positive self-image.
- Reduces your dependence on getting other people's approval.
- 'Gets the cards on the table,' clarifying issues so that everyone knows where they stand.
- Increases the likelihood that both sides in a conflict will realize at least some of their goals.
- Improves problem-solving and decision-making because more people present ideas and bad decisions are less likely to go through by default.

But if assertiveness isn't balanced by responsiveness to the needs of others, it turns into power-play, or dominance. Of course, situations exist in which arbitrary, macho or aggressively imposed solutions to conflict have a role. Emergencies may not allow you the luxury of consultation before decisions have to be made. Also, a long-running conflict between members of a team

FIGURE 4: Four approaches to handling conflict situations

AVOIDANCE Unassertive Unresponsive	COLLABORATION **Assertive** **Responsive**
DOMINANCE **Assertive** Unresponsive	ACCOMMODATION Unassertive **Responsive**

may require the team-leader to impose solutions neither side would have chosen voluntarily. In some instances people have been found to like 'strong leadership' because it provides feelings of security, builds a common bond, and saves individuals the effort of thinking for themselves.

But although dominance can produce short-term positive results, it does so only by adding a second conflict to the first one. In the long-term, aggressive or dominant leadership seldom wins hearts. People may accept imposed solutions to conflict, but they won't always internalize them or act on them. In other words, dominant behavior may be ineffective in transferring goals, in motivating, and in creating commitment. Over the long haul, in fact, the dominant style will eventuate in bitterness, hostility, intransigence, attempts at sabotage, or a stultifying submission and dependence.

Accommodation

The converse of dominance is accommodation. You become accommodating by responding to the needs of others without asserting needs of your own. Not surprisingly this is associated with *concessionary* bargaining, just as dominance is associated with *combative* bargaining. It also features strongly in Eastern, and particularly Japanese, expressions of deference shown by junior to senior managers.

Clearly there are benefits in being able to sacrifice your own needs to those of others, and this is one of the reasons why accommodation is a feature of hierarchical systems of management. People know which side their bread is buttered on. Also, being the net giver in a relationship gives you the satisfaction of occupying the moral high ground, since nobody can accuse you of making unreasonable demands, and most people will see you as concerned and helpful. This veneer of high principle, though, too often masks an inability to engage with a real underlying conflict. It's worth remembering that being accommodating:

■ Isn't the same as being polite – you can be polite and assertive at the same time.
■ Can make you go overboard by trying to meet needs that others in reality do not have.
■ Isn't the only alternative to dominance and aggression.
■ Often reflects anxiety over confrontation, and a fear that assertive behavior will bring disapproval and rejection by others, or cause you to look foolish or stupid.

Accommodation reduces anxiety by nullifying conflict. In practice this usually means appeasing others and falling in behind them, for which you receive an immediate reward in the form of praise for your selflessness and readiness not to rock the boat. In the long run, however, the persistent denial of personal need and the persistent failure to reach personal goals will have a damaging effect. It will produce a progressive loss of self-esteem, a growing sense of hurt and anger, and, eventually, an explosion of resentment which revives the original conflict in a more extreme expression.

Avoidance

Avoidance entails a total failure to engage with conflict. You are neither assertive (defending your own interests) nor responsive (taking account of the interests of others). The strategy takes various forms. People practice *evasion* – refusing to acknowledge that the conflict exists. They *withdraw* – physically absenting themselves from the scene of the conflict, so they don't have to 'get involved'. If a discussion is moving towards disagreement, they *close off* – changing the subject, or quickly terminating the conversation.

In the short-term, there may be good reasons for doing this. For example, when:

▪ Engaging with the conflict would make matters worse.
▪ There is insufficient time to deal with the conflict.
▪ The conflict concerns a minor issue and other matters are more pressing.

In this sense, avoidance is part of prioritization: you have to deal with things in order of urgency and importance, and at moments when there seems a reasonable chance of resolving them. At the same time, avoidance seldom if ever works as a long-term tactic against conflict. Most grievances do not just go away. Your refusing to discuss a problem will introduce into the other person's mind a suspicion that you're not really interested. And total breakdown of communication – where two people aren't talking to one another – can bury a relationship in a rut from which they will have great difficulty rescuing it. In addition to which the avoidance tactic seriously reduces your power to influence and control events going on around you. Staying aloof may satisfy some ego-needs, but it does so at the cost of your ability to achieve real results.

Collaboration

Fully expressing your viewpoint, and fully responding to that of the other party, provides the only real foundation for win-win solutions to relationship breakdown.

If you suspect your sales team failed to reach its planned objectives through lack of support from your line manager, you can deal with the situation in one of four ways. Through *avoidance* – pretending the problem doesn't exist. Through *accommodation* – letting your people take the rap in order the shield the superior. Through *dominance* – directly or indirectly heaping blame on your manager without hearing his or her side of the story. Or through *collaboration* – going in and beginning a dialogue: 'We had some disappointing results last quarter, and I think one of the ways we could turn that around is by looking at the way we're communicating down the management line ...'

A number of approaches help in taking a collaborative approach to conflict:

■ **SEE DIFFERENCE AS VALUABLE.** Always try to remember that conflict is a healthy sign. Companies where people never disagree are liable to become flabby and complacent. So the fact that someone takes a view different from yours, or has a different kind of personality, provides a powerful asset for you to work on.

■ **ACT EARLY.** If you suspect a relationship is going wrong, don't just sit back and watch it unravel. Every unresolved disagreement you rack up with another person becomes part of the history of that relationship, and the longer the conflict is left unattended, the more it becomes the 'reality' and the harder it is to turn around. Don't allow people to catch the habit of enmity by failing to intervene in time.

■ **NEVER GOSSIP OR CRITICIZE BEHIND SOMEONE'S BACK.** This is an absolute no-no. Once you've 'politicized' the breakdown of a relationship by forcing others to take sides, you considerably reduce the chances of getting that relationship back on track. Even the most trusted confidants can be indiscreet, and once the rumor of a remark you've made starts circulating on the grapevine, there's no way to rescind it. If you have to let off steam about a colleague (and most of us do), choose someone outside the workplace who doesn't have to relate to people you both know.

■ **LOOK AT THE FACTS**. No two people see a situation in exactly the same way, nor is either likely to see the situation in its entirety. Conflict can arise simply out of the fact that two people are working from different perceptions of the same set of facts. Also, once a conflict has begun, the actual differences that gave rise to the conflict get displaced by more emotive and less verifiable ones based on what one party *thinks* the other is doing. Always make sure a grievance has its roots in tangible events you can pin down through objective investigation. The correct response to 'I feel you're being unfair to me' is 'Give me an example so that we can talk about specific instances.'

■ **DON'T BE AFRAID OF FEELINGS**. It's perfectly acceptable to tell people how you feel. 'I feel very disappointed that you acted in this way,' for instance, or, 'When I heard about this it made me angry.' But that doesn't mean you should present your case in an emotive way. Displays of frustration, anger, fear, anxiety or distress usually alienate people, cloud the issue, prevent effective listening, and deepen rather than resolve the conflict.

■ **ADDRESS DEEP ISSUES, NOT JUST TRIGGERS**. Remember that underlying causes of conflict will persist unless they are tackled head-on. In a case of prejudice, for example, the real problem isn't the offensive remark that prompts a complaint, but the attitude of the person who made it. Causes may be harder to treat than symptoms, but if you don't treat them the same symptoms will keep on recurring.

■ **LOOK FOR THE TRUTH IN WHAT OTHERS SAY**. In a disagreement most people think first about proving their own point of view. Conflicts, though, rarely appear out of thin air. If handled properly, discussion of someone else's grievance against you can provide a useful opportunity for self-assessment. Try to be objective. Don't be afraid of admitting you've made a mistake. Nobody's perfect, and other people in the organization will appreciate honesty. Coming clean actually saves face on both sides. The other person will feel vindicated, and you'll win respect for your frankness. People spend so much of their time being defensive that when somebody else takes the rap the usual response is gratitude and relief.

■ **CALL IN A MEDIATOR.** Honest brokers can play a vital role in restoring a relationship. Standing outside, they cannot be accused of partiality. And the other party can listen to them, talk to them, and defer to their judgement in a way that would be impossible in a one-on-one confrontation. For most situations it's best to suggest informal mediation using a trusted mutual acquaintance who has the sensitivity and skill to draw the issues out.

■ **PRIORITIZE A BROKEN RELATIONSHIP.** Very often relationship breakdown worsens when the two parties don't really know each other or have 'lost touch.' To prevent a resolved conflict resurfacing, make an effort to get to know the other person better and to put the relationship on a more personal footing. Trust and confidence flow from contact. A relaxed lunch or a game of softball can have surprising effects.

You won't be able to solve every conflict point by point. In some cases conflicts arise because two people are being made to compete for the same resources. Department heads sometimes find themselves in a struggle over budget allocations. Members of a sales team may be chasing the same finite customer base. In such zero-sum negotiations, where one person can only gain at the expense of another, it's best to look at organizational options for reducing conflict by changing the rules of the game – for instance, by basing commission on team performance rather than individual performance.

If that's impossible, collaboration may boil down to compromise. Both sides get part of what they want, but only part. Compromise should not be seen as a dirty word. But its weaknesses should be borne in mind. One of these is that compromise resolves conflict only so long as both parties continue to see the solution as fair. If my department budget remains static while my department costs increase relative to those of other department heads, conflict re-emerges and a new round of negotiation will ensue.

Summary and action plan

Conflict is the reality in relationships. We have been conditioned to think of conflict as a negative trait, to be rooted out and eradicated. In fact, though, a relationship without conflict is a relationship without stimulation and creative drive. The question isn't how we can get rid of conflict, but how we can redirect energies to a productive end.

It's worth noting that relationships across cultural boundaries break down so much more frequently than others simply because the opportunities for conflict are more numerous. Apparently our instinctive reactions to difference are suspicion, caution and hostility. Yet the difficulties of relating cross-culturally are mirrored by the extent of the rewards available to those who get cross-cultural relationships to fly. When it works, the culturally mixed team commands a formidable breadth of outlook, experience and expertise. In an age where globalism demands cross-cultural cooperation, it will become progressively more important to handle conflict in a constructive way.

Finally, then, a check-list for conflict utilization includes the following:

1 Think through what the motive forces behind the conflict are – whether they are rooted in style issues, values, prejudice, self-esteem, dependency or tribalism.
2 Try to discern what positive qualities drive the conflict and which can be redirected to more productive uses.

3 Evaluate to what extent you are being assertive and responsive in your approach to resolving the conflict, and whether your current strategies are geared to the short or the long term.

4 Ask yourself whether resolving the problem requires the involvement of a mediator, and who might be able to perform this function effectively.

5 Find informal ways to build the relationship outside the context of task-driven interaction.

Notes

[1] Akio Morita with Edwin M. Reingold and Mitsuko Shimomun, *Made in Japan: Akio Morita and Sony* (London: Collins, 1987), p.146.

[2] Morita with Reingold and Shimomun, *Made in Japan*, p.147.

[3] P.D. Grub and J.H. Lin, *Foreign Direct Investment in China* (New York: Quorum Books, 1991).

[4] J. Mann, *Beijing Jeep: The Short, Unhappy Romance of American Business in China* (New York: Simon & Schuster, 1989).

Index